Regency Furniture

THE DRAWING-ROOM AT SOUTHILL FINISHED AND FURNISHED SOON AFTER 1800.

REGENCY FURNITURE

1795—1820

by

MARGARET JOURDAIN

LONDON: COUNTRY LIFE LTD.

2-10 Tavistock Street, Covent Garden, W.C.2

NEW YORK: CHARLES SCRIBNER'S SONS

First Published in 1934
Revised and enlarged Edition 1948

PRINTED IN GREAT BRITAIN BY ROBERT MACLEHOSE AND CO. LTD.
THE UNIVERSITY PRESS, GLASGOW

Contents

List of Illustrations

List of Illustrations

List of Illustrations

List of Illustrations

List of Illustrations

. xi .

List of Illustrations

Preface

The term Regency as now applied to the decorative arts in England overlaps the short period when George, Prince of Wales, was Regent, and covers all the work in the new classic style a decade before the institution of the Regency in 1811, and after his accession as George IV in 1820. It is a more acceptable title than 'English Empire', for the English classic is not a close version of, but an offshoot from, the French Imperial style. The new style was not derived from the taste of the Prince of Wales, whose leanings were towards oriental lacquer and lavish gilding, and the overcharged and dazzling splendour at Windsor Castle was, it is said, 'his Majesty's taste'.[1]

The style was for long termed 'English Empire', a description which indicates its debt to France. The style of Louis XVI was the last to follow in architecture the quest of recapturing the spirit of antiquity, and of using and adapting its ornament by a process of selection. Revolutionary France[2] led the way in a new classical movement, aiming at a close reproduction of ancient monuments, or when this was not possible, of such portions of these as could be adapted.

The French version of the classic style which reached its zenith under Napoleon, became part of the artistic heritage of the European countries which had formed the Napoleonic Empire, Holland, Italy and Spain; and Sweden and Germany adopted it with little modification.

The aim of the leading artists and decorators was the union of architecture, decoration and furnishing. 'Furniture is too closely connected (according to Percier and Fontaine, arbiters of taste in France, whose *Recueil de decorations intérieures* was widely read) for the architect to remain indifferent to it. Construction and decoration are in close relation, and if they cease to appear so, there is a flaw in the whole.' In the French classical revival it was admitted that the rigid imitation of antiquity

---

[1] C. B. Wollaston, who saw Windsor Castle in 1828, noticed the 'dazzling splendour of the gilding, which seems to be much overdone', and Mr. W——ville said it was 'His Majesty's taste'.—*Journal of Mary Frampton*, p. 337.

[2] The dates of French political changes are:
> Directoire, 1795–1799.
> Napoleon, first consul, 1799–1805.
> Napoleon, emperor, 1805–1814.

. xiii .

was impossible, and Fontaine recognised that a compromise was necessary. 'We have followed the models of antiquity (he writes) not blindly, but with the discrimination entailed by the manners, customs, and materials of the moderns'. Symbols from Roman antiquity were used as relevant to the Napoleonic present; the nation's pride showed itself as the figures of winged victories; the sphinxes served to recall the delusive successes of 1798 in Egypt; and Roman weapons and shields summoned up associations of 'ancient virtue'.

In England the style can be seen in being in Sheraton's first book of designs (*The Cabinet-makers and Upholsterers' Drawing Book*, 1791–4) and is well-marked in his *Cabinet Dictionary* which was issued in 1803. The debt to the French Empire style is not so large as in other countries of Western Europe, and certain designers, for instance, Charles Heathcote Tatham and Thomas Hope, studied antiquity at first hand in Italy. The most gifted exponent of the early phase of the style was the architect Henry Holland, who altered and enlarged Carlton House for the Prince of Wales, 'improved' Woburn for the Duke of Bedford, recased and redecorated much of Althorp for Lord Spencer, and altered and decorated Southill for Samuel Whitbread.[1] He borrowed elements from the French Directoire style, and employed a number of French craftsmen, painters and metal workers who found employment at a standstill in France during the Revolution and the Directory. After Holland's death in 1806, design stiffened in the grip of an uncompromising classicism, borrowing from the marble and metal remains preserved and excavated in Italy.

Samuel Rogers's home in St. James's Square was entirely 'Grecian', and one of the most striking features of the house was its large collection of Greek vases.[2] In Sir Edward Lytton Bulwer's house in Charles Street, one of the drawing-rooms was a facsimile of a chamber he had visited at Pompeii, with vases, candelabra, chairs and tables in the Pompeian taste;[3] Thomas Hope's interiors at Deepdene were a consistent archaeological fantasy recorded in his *Household Furniture* (1807). Numerous pieces of Roman bronze furniture and parts of furniture have been preserved, especially from Pompeii, including couches, low stools, tripods and lamp-stands, dating chiefly from the time of the Emperors. The designers of the Regency transformed these forms of Roman bronze and marble into *wooden* furniture.

The Regency period was subject to swift and changeful currents in design.

---

[1] Holland's work at Carlton House dates from 1788. In 1789 he 'improved' Woburn; and his alterations to Althorp were completed in 1790.

[2] Clayden, *Early Life of Samuel Rogers*, Vol. I, pp. 448–9. [3] G. Church, *Mayfair and Belgravia* (1892), p. 102.

Preface

Many pieces of furniture, in the words of the author of the *New Circle of the Mechanical Arts* (1819) were 'daily falling into disuse, while others are introduced which, for a time, are considered indispensably necessary for our comfort'. The novelty and ingenuity of patents and forms is constantly emphasised. The later phase of Regency design is less happy, and as it developed, there was a greater profusion of ornament, and an increasing bulk which allowed more surface to be enriched.

Regency design has had an influence upon modern work. 'They were the modernists of a hundred and thirty years ago', as Mr. Christopher Hussey writes, 'and were actuated by the same impatience with triviality that has stimulated their modern successors, seeking the same remedies in solidity and simplicity to which Parisian *ensembliers* have had recourse.'[1] There is the same accent on what Hope aimed at, 'breadth and repose of surface,' 'distinctness and contrast of outline,' and 'the opposition of plain and enriched parts.' Strictly speaking, 'Regency' might be applied only to those innovators, but in practice it is also used to cover a type of furniture which is not 'new' or classical, but is a simplification of the eighteenth century tradition.

Not a little of the interest of 'Regency' work lies in the similarity of outlook in the designers of that period and their modern successors. 'In each case the designers have been actuated by the same desire: to evolve a form which shall owe as little as possible to precedent and custom, but satisfy by its compactness, sanity and sound use of materials.' In each case the designer accepts the advantages of machine-simplification.[2]

[1] C. Hussey, *Country Life*, Dec. 7, 1929.   [2] *I.e.* in Regency furniture, the use of cast metal mounts.

LONDON,   MARGARET JOURDAIN.
1947.

The Greek Revival

England in the early nineteenth century was dazzled by that 'point of light in history', ancient Greece. Even before the opening of this century, Charles Heathcote Tatham writes to Holland of the interest in Greek architecture which is gaining ground in England. Early in the nineteenth century in almost all new buildings Grecian members and ornaments were 'so prevalent as to obtrude themselves upon the notice of the most superficial observer'.[1] Greek ornament was to be found in the houses of men of taste; and when Samuel Rogers bought a house in St. James's Square in 1802, 'Greek vases dotted the house; much of the furniture was modelled on the same classic source, and the staircase was decorated with a frieze copied from a famous original among the Elgin marbles.'

The leading architect in this transitional period was Henry Holland, who beginning in the Adam tradition, developed his style in the direction of the French version of classicism, and shows in his interior decoration and furniture a delicacy of invention that cannot be matched in the work of any other architect of this period. In a book of office drawings in the library of the Royal Institute of British Architects there are sketches for furniture, mirrors and pier tables, and a bookcase for the library at Woburn, and also drawings for bookcases for Debden Hall (1796). In the alterations and redecorations undertaken by him for the Whig noblemen of the day —Lord Palmerston at Broadlands, and Lord Spencer at Althorp—the same sane taste is visible which marks his work at Carlton House.[2] During the last phase—the decade before his death—he was 'the most open of architects then working, to French fashions'. It was his Gallican—or as the Tories considered, Jacobin—bias that made him so acceptable to the Carlton House coterie.[3]

Holland was a brilliant decorative artist whose work is often a 'perfect combination of the requirements of eye and use'. There was in most of what he designed an assured distinction only to be matched in the contemporary French decorative arts. His style is to be seen in the furniture at Southill designed for Samuel Whitbread, and also in the furniture made for Carlton House during the last few years of the

---

[1] Busby, *Villas and Country Houses*, 1808.

[2] Henry Holland was architect to the Prince of Wales until his death in 1806.   [3] *Country Life*, Nov. 9, 1929.

eighteenth century (Figs. 1-4 and 6-10). Closely associated with Holland is Charles Heathcote Tatham[1] (1771–1842), (brother of the cabinet-maker Thomas Tatham), an architect who had been sent by Holland to make drawings in Rome of classic detail to be used at Carlton House. The fruits of his stay are contained in several works published between 1796 and 1799, such as the etchings representing the best examples of ancient ornamental architecture. To him the writer of the Architectural Publications Society's *Dictionary* assigns a large share in the rise of the Anglo-Greek style.

Holland who was engaged to transform and redecorate the existing house at Southill inherited by Samuel Whitbread in 1796, was paid in 1801 £200 as 'commission on furniture', and some of his drawings for the Southill furniture are preserved in the Library of the Royal Institute of British Architects. 'The Southill accounts show an average yearly expenditure on furniture over the whole period from 1796 to Samuel Whitbread's death in 1815 of some £1,000. In the peak period, 1800 to 1802 the yearly average was two and a half times as high. From 1803 to 1808 it dropped far below the average.'[2]

In the furniture of this early period, the material employed is a dark wood, such as rosewood, kingwood or mahogany, which throws up the finished brass or ormolu mounts and mouldings (Figs. 3-5 and 9-11). The mouldings are sometimes emphasised by the juxtaposition of ebonised bandings. The detail, such as the anthemium and the acanthus spray, is drawn from Greek ornament(Fig. 8). The French influence is traceable in certain forms, such as the shelved commode (Fig. 10) and the slender ormolu colonnettes at the corners of the rosewood china cabinet (Fig. 3). In the lady's writing-table, the rectilinear severity of the supports is relieved by the carved and gilt Greek detail of the feet and the ormolu ornaments applied to the supports (Fig. 2).

While Southill has the richest equipment of Holland's furniture, there are pieces made originally for Carlton House, in which there is the same characteristic abstemiousness and effective Greek detail. The closest approximation to the Empire style are the rosewood bookcases in the Regency Room, Buckingham Palace (Fig. 11); the ormolu mounts in these, and in two larger bookcases by the same firm, are unusually varied, and it is probable that some French founder, such as Dominique, was employed. The bookcases were made by Marsh and Tatham, who in 1806 supplied several for Carlton House with 'rich ormolu mounts, ormolu ornaments, and plate glass and statuary ledges for the same'.[3]

[1] Information supplied by Mr. H. Clifford Smith.   [2] Note from Mr. Humphrey Whitbread.

[3] H. C. Smith, *Buckingham Palace* (1931), p. 23.

The Greek Revival

In some furniture formerly at Hartwell[1] there is a close stylistic resemblance to some pieces at Southill; and they must be by the same maker.

It is unfortunate that Holland died at the time when the revived classicism had established itself. No example of this 'English *directoire*' can be dated later than 1806 (the year of his death), and in the following year the classical revival was given a new direction by the *Household Furniture* of Thomas Hope.

The successive stages of the Greek taste are recorded in publications which exhibit clearly the character of the revival, and the point at which it overweights the sense of form and becomes antiquarian. A young artist, Moses, was encouraged by the success of Tatham's etchings of ancient ornament to bring out his less expensive collection of antique vases, altars, paterae, tripods and candelabra in 1812. Richardson's collection of ornaments in the antique style was published in 1815. Ackermann's *Ornaments for the Use of Sculptors, Painters and Modellers*, which was published in 1827, is based entirely on Greek detail. In a design for a pedestal by Richard Brown, in his *Rudiments of Drawing Cabinet and Upholstery Furniture* (1820) the brass ornament on the standard is taken from the cornice of the Parthenon, and another design stated to be 'the result of the author's study of Greek and Roman examples'. In 1822, it was said that the English 'is more chaste than the French Greek, and has advanced so rapidly during the last ten years that the French have adopted much of it'.[2]

This idealisation of Greece was expressed by emphasising the elements of severity in furniture. As an archaeological reconstruction of Greek or Roman furniture was impossible, designers compromised, adapting the forms to serve the uses of the modern world. In France, Fontaine, who collaborated with Percier, wrote that they 'have followed the models of antiquity not blindly, but with discrimination entailed by the manners, customs and materials of the moderns'. Classical types of furniture were, however, closely followed, such as the couch, the cross-framed chair and stool, and the round table with lion feet.

Chairs, both in England and on the Continent, were by 1802 'of different shapes and patterns copied after the antique'. The bosses applied to the junction of the leg and seat rail in imitation of bolt heads suggest the influence of classical furniture. The maker of the two gilt council chairs from Carlton House is unknown (Fig. 29).

---

[1] These pieces were made for William Lee Antonie of Colworth, member for Bedford, and friend of Samuel Whitbread of Southill.

[2] Cited in Architectural Publication Society's *Dictionary*, under Furniture.

Regency Furniture

The backs are solid to the ground and carved with Greek acanthus scrolls repeated on either side of a vertical line, and each of the front supports is composed of a winged sphinx. They resemble the marble thrones with solid sides and animal and sphinx supports of which Charles Heathcote Tatham published illustrations in his *Ancient Ornamental Architecture*.[1]

The word 'Grecian' becomes part of the furniture-maker's vocabulary, and many of the sumptuous and costly pieces of furniture now in the state-rooms of Buckingham Palace, which can be dated by the Royal accounts, are severely classic in form or detail or in both. Examples of this classic furniture are the candelabra made by Tatham in 1811,[2] and the set of gilt settees made in 1810 by Tatham and Bailey for the crimson drawing-room at Carlton House.[3]

In architecture and furniture the aim was an extreme simplicity of form, with a partiality for large uninterrupted surfaces, unbroken lines and bold curves, and the reduction of ornament to a minor role.

The lion foot and lion monopodium and the lyre are also legacies from the classic antiquity. No detail was used more frequently than reeding, which emphasises structural lines, whether vertical or horizontal. The careful drawing of the acanthus leaves upon the wine-cooler (Fig. 172) and supports to the dining table from the Liverpool Town Hall is also characteristic of this revivalist furniture.

There is an increasing use of Greek *motifs* during the early nineteenth century. In Brown's *Rudiments*[4] and Nicholson's *Practical Cabinet-maker*, much of the detail is of Greek origin, and a selection of ornaments from the safest and 'chastest' Greek sources is also supplied.

Illustrations pp. 58-64.

---

[1] Such as the 'grand antique chair in Parian marble' in the Vatican Museum (Plate 84). In the Louvre is a marble seat supported by winged female sphinxes. Cf. Ransom, *Ancient Furniture* (Fig. 281).

[2] H. C. Smith, *Buckingham Palace*, Figs. 158 and 159.   [3] *Ibid.*, Fig. 177.

[4] *Rudiments of Drawing Cabinet Furniture*, 1820.

Furniture of Thomas Hope

Thomas Hope,[1] the banker and virtuoso, the eldest of the sons of John Hope of Amsterdam the descendant of a family of Amsterdam merchants, is an influential figure in the development of the classical revival and introduced severer forms in furniture. After a childhood spent in Holland, he came to London, where he had been preceded by other members of the Hope family, who had fled from their Dutch homes in fear of the French invasion of 1794.[2] As a young man he had had some architectural training, and prior to his arrival in England he had spent eight years in studying architectural remains in Greece, Turkey, Asia Minor, Syria and Egypt. Five volumes of his original drawings exist, containing a record of the antiquities of the Eastern Mediterranean at the close of the eighteenth century. His friendship with the French architect Percier brought him under the influence of a designer who, with his friend Fontaine, had given a definite classic form to the 'Empire' style; and his personal taste[3] inclined towards the rigidity of the new style. The interiors of Hope's London house in Duchess Street and at Deepdene in Surrey, designed as backgrounds for his collection of Egyptian and Roman sculptures, vases and objects of art, were an archaeological fantasy, the product of some learning and much enthusiasm. Whatever setting he chose, Greek, Roman or Egyptian, the scheme was carried out with consistent zeal.

Hope does not appear to have pushed his theories except by the issue of his *Household Furniture* (1807), for which he made most of the drawings. In it he writes that cabinet-makers had even before its publication directly imitated his furniture, that 'extravagant caricatures' had 'started up in every corner of the capital'.[4] He pleads for 'that breadth and repose of surface . . . that harmony and significance of accessories, and that apt accord between the peculiar meaning of each imitative or significant detail and the peculiar destination of the main object to which these accessories belonged, which are calculated to afford to the eye and mind the most

---

[1] 1769–1831.   [2] Law, *Book of the Beresford Hopes.*

[3] He writes: 'I scarcely was able to hold a pencil when . . . I already began dealing with those straight lines which seem so little attractive to the general number,' *An Historical Essay on Architecture*, (2nd ed., 1835), p. 183.

[4] *Household Furniture* (1807), p. 11.

lively, most permanent and most unfading enjoyment'.[1] It was a scholar's plea, and at Deepdene his system of significant detail was carried out. The London house was complete in 1804, when Dance, who visited it, was of the opinion that ' by the singularity of it, good might be done, as it might contribute to emancipate the public taste from that rigid adherence to a certain style of architecture and of finishing, and unshackle the artist'. The 'singularity' of the new classic movement lay in a close and archaeological reproduction of Roman furniture.[2] In his *Household Furniture*, Hope illustrates a table of his design supported by 'chimaeras in bronze, similar to some limbs of ideal animals adapted to the same purpose, which have been found among the remains of Pompeii'. Preoccupied with this ideal severity, Hope aimed at making objects of modern use, a fire-screen, a bookcase and a sideboard, congruous with the Roman tradition. In this he was successful; his new designs *were* congruous with the classic, and the ornamental detail consistently applied. Hope's achievement can be studied in his *Household Furniture*, which is a record of the decoration and furniture of his Surrey house, Deepdene, which remained practically undisturbed until 1917. Examples of Hope's work are the bookcase in the Egyptian taste (Fig. 14) the table with its top inlaid with ebony and silver (Fig. 15, 16) and the stands supported by lion monopodia (Fig. 17).

There is a marked change in the temper of criticism from the date of the publication of his *Household Furniture* to the second decade of the nineteenth century. His *Household Furniture* was at first ridiculed in the *Edinburgh Review*[3] as frivolous, and George Dance's[4] reaction on seeing Hope's London house in 1804 was 'amusement'. The reviewer's criticism of the weak points of Hope's design, such as its bulkiness, is to the point. It was 'too bulky, massive and ponderous to be commodious for general use', an 'assemblage of squared timber and massive brass as would weigh down the floor and crush out the walls of an ordinary London house'. But in the full tide of the Greek revival, his innovations were accepted as 'the beautifully classic change'.[5]

Illustrations pp. 65-68.

[1] *Ibid.*, p. 2.   [2] 'Mr. Hope's house resembled a museum'—*Farington Diary*, Oct. 23, 1812.
[3] 1807, Vol. X, 478.   [4] *Farington Diary*, March 31, 1804.
[5] J. T. Smith, *Nollekens and His Times*. (Ed. Whitten) Vol. I, p. 175, 1920.

The Egyptian Revival

A short-lived attempt to naturalise Egyptian motives and symbolism (and in a few cases, architectural forms) dates from the first years of the nineteenth century. This revival follows upon Bonaparte's expedition to Syria and Egypt in 1798–1801, in which an archaeological mission duplicated Bonaparte's military staff. Since this expedition interest was aroused in the art of Egypt, as surpassing in grandeur and strangeness any other of the visible works of man. After the campaign, Vivant Denon, the leading archaeologist of the expedition, had a bedroom fitted up by Jacob Desmalter to his own design in the Egyptian style. The bed, which was of mahogany inlaid with silver, had three sides ornamented with bas-reliefs of kneeling figures; its head was decorated with a carved Isis and the legs with the Uraeus.

Egyptian detail is figured in Percier and Fontaine's *Recueil* (1812) and introduced in their decorations for Napoleon as first Consul; and Farrington, who visited Paris in 1802, noticed in Napoleon's private apartment in the Tuileries that 'the Egyptian figure of the Sphinx made part of the framework of the chairs in one of the apartments'.[1]

Archaeologists and travellers, such as Volney[2] and Grohmann, had led the way in the exploration of Egypt during the late years of the eighteenth century and Piranesi[3] had used Egyptian *motifs* in his designs, maintaining that what had been called its rigidity and harshness was only a sign of the 'harmonious force and solidity' of the style. To the influence of these early pioneers must be assigned the silver candelabrum and a pair of candlesticks bearing the London hallmarks for the years 1791–1792.[4]

It was, however, not until the publication of Denon's *Voyages dans la Basse et Haute Égypte* in 1802 that this archaeological revival had any large following in England. Its publication 'gave use and life to a taste for this description of embellishment'.[5] Its progress in this country (which also had its share in the Egyptian

---

[1] *Diary*, September, 1802.

[2] Volney, *Voyage en Égypte* (1787). Translation of Norden's *Voyage d'Égypte et de Nubie* (1795). Grohmann, *Restes d'architecture Égyptienne* (1799).

[3] *Diverse maniere d'adornare i camini*, Plate 14. [4] Jackson, *Illustrated History of English Plate*, Vol. II, p. 875.

[5] G. Smith, *Cabinet-makers' and Upholsterers' Guide* (1826), p. vi.

campaign) is recorded in magazines and architectural publications. By 1806 it had affected 'many articles of interior decoration' and had become the 'present prevailing fashion'.[1] It was experimented in by Thomas Hope[2] (who had sketched the antiquities of Egypt for the room in which his collection of Egyptian antiquities were housed. The decoration, designed to 'bear some analogy to its contents', was taken from Egyptian mummy cases and papyri, the colouring of the walls, ceiling and furniture pale yellow and bluish green, relieved by masses of black and gold. He was considered to have 'made a perfect hieroglyphic of most of our apartments'.[3] Hope warns the 'young artist' that this style is not to be lightly undertaken, 'the hieroglyphic figures, so universally employed by the Egyptians, can afford us little pleasure on account of their meaning since this is seldom intelligible'.

In spite of Hope's warning, Egyptian detail became the vogue. At Crawley House, in Bedfordshire, the wallpaper of the drawing-room preserves its borders in which a mummy serves as a 'stop' to divide two sphinxes, and a chimney-glass in the same room is decorated with a lotus and anthemium frieze and 'Egyptian female heads to the pilasters', as entered in the upholsterer Collis's bill in 1806. At Harewood House, in Yorkshire, according to the *Tourist's Companion* (1819)[4] the entrance hall was 'fitted up in the Egyptian style', and in a description of White Knights, published in the same year, one room is described as 'ornamented with a painted cornice and capitals in the Egyptian manner', while the chimneypiece was 'sculptured in the same style of art, each side being supported by an Isis'.

A bookcase from Deepdene (Fig. 14), designed by Hope in the Egyptian manner, has the entablature supported by pilasters terminating in Egyptian heads, while the supports to the lower stage are lion-headed.

At Stourhead in Wiltshire is a quantity of furniture in mahogany and satinwood made by the younger Thomas Chippendale for the Wiltshire antiquary, Sir Richard Colt Hoare, in the early years of the nineteenth century. Among the bills is an entry of a set of 'eight mahogany chairs with circular backs, broad sweep pannelled tops, with circle elbows, carved Egyptian heads and fluted therm feet, the rails moulded and carved, cane seats and brass socket castors' for the library, and the mahogany table and pedestal writing table are also enriched with Egyptian, combined, in the case of the writing-table, with classic heads (Fig. 127). The tapering and fluted sheaths

[1] J. Randall, *A Collection of Architectural Designs for Mansions* (1806).

[2] In the bibliography in his *Household Furniture* Hope mentions Denon's work and Norden's *Egypt* among the works which had been most useful to him.

[3] *Edinburgh Review* (1807), Vol. X, p. 485.   [4] Jewell, *Tourist's Companion*, 1819, p. 21.

finish below in human feet, both in the engaged supports upon the front of the table and in the free-standing Egyptian supports between the plinth and semi-circular ends. The finely-finished heads are carved, not inserted in cast brass which became customary in furniture of this type.

A silver candelabrum in this style, which was made for the Duke of Cumberland in 1805, has the shaft in the form of a triform Egyptian figure resting on a triangular base supported by winged sphinxes. The candle branches are shaped as foliated scrolls terminating in dolphin heads (Fig. 206).

That the Egyptian style did not stop short at archaeological *motifs* we have the evidence of a description of a house in *Our Village*, in which the library is Egyptian, 'all covered with hieroglyphics and swarming with furniture crocodiles and Sphinxes.'[1] The sofa (Fig. 20), a piece of sheer extravagance which might have come from this library, is an unique survival of this swarm.

Illustrations pp. 69-71.

[1] 'Only think of a crocodile couch and a Sphinx sofa,' Miss Mitford, *Our Village*, Vol. IV, p. 239–40.

The Chinese Taste

'Even the grotesque has its beauty' (so runs a passage in the English test of Piranesi's *Diverse maniere d'adornare i camini*),[1] and therefore, though the Chinese taste was admittedly 'far distant from the Grecian and perhaps more so than the Egyptian and Tuscan, we are delighted to have our rooms and apartments fitted up after the Chinese manner'.

China, an object of curiosity intermittently through three centuries, was known by drawings in books of travel, but Sir William Chambers's *Designs for Chinese Buildings*, du Halde's great work on the Chinese empire,[2] the embassy of Lord Macartney in 1792–1794, has enlightened and clarified English taste. The attraction of Chinese art was readily comprehensible. It was an art of exquisite finish (but not to the European eye consistent), it was an escape from the discipline of the five orders.

Interest in Chinese art which was revived just before the middle of the eighteenth century, continued in a crescendo of fashionable whim and caprice until the classical revival under Robert Adam. The style thus established as a fashion was constantly ridiculed in the mid-eighteenth century, and in a discussion of its merits by Alison in his *Essays on Taste*, the admiration of the 'fantastic and uncouth' forms of this Anglo-Oriental art is explained as due to association. 'They were universally admired because they brought to mind those images of Eastern magnificence and splendour of which we have heard so much, and which we are always willing to believe because they are distant.'[3] an example of the romantic fallacy which idealises the distant, both in time and place, and identifies beauty with the unfamiliar.[4]

The last revival during the Regency owes something to the personal taste of George IV when Prince of Wales. When alterations were being made in the Brighton Pavilion in 1802, 'several pieces of very beautiful Chinese paper were presented to the Prince, who for a time was undecided in what way to make use of them. Finally

---

[1] *Diversi maniere d'adornare i camini*, 1769, p. 10.
[2] J. B. Du Halde, *Description de l'Empire de la Chine*, 1735.
[3] Archibald Alison, *Essays on Taste* (1815 edition), p. 195.
[4] See Geoffrey Scott, *The Architecture of Humanism*, p. 39.

they were hung in a Chinese gallery, and the other parts of the gallery painted and decorated in a corresponding style.'[1]

Much of the interior of the Pavilion, with its palm tree columns, and 'the fantastic forms that raise themselves with the bravest fanfares of rhetoric',[2] witnesses to the Prince of Wales's experiments in this novel version of the Chinese taste.

That the Chinese taste had already caught the Prince of Wales's taste before that date there is the evidence in his Chinese drawing-room at Carlton House, described and illustrated by Sheraton in his *Cabinet Makers' and Upholsterers' Drawing-book*. The walls of the room are divided by 'Chinese columns' and the panels painted with 'Chinese views and little scenes'. The marble chimneypiece and two marble-topped pier-tables and two shelved side-tables have been identified as designed by Henry Holland about 1790 for the Prince's Chinese room[3]. The pair of pier-tables in the yellow drawing-room at Buckingham Palace are surmounted by marble slabs and supported by four terminal figures of Chinamen in painted and gilt bronze; the framework of the table is of ebony mounted with ormolu (Fig.24). A second pair of marble-topped pier-tables in the principal corridor is also of ebony, veneered upon pine and mounted with ormolu. The ends are shelved, the open centre mounted in ormolu with a fringed drapery held up on each side by a dragon (Fig. 23). Holland's *Chinoiseries* were quite independent of and a foil to his developed style. The taste for 'Chinese' furniture was carried on for the decoration of the Brighton Pavilion when it took its final form from 1815 to 1822, and was chiefly carried out by the firm of Crace and Robert Jones. Among furniture designed by Robert Jones, and carried out by Bailey & Saunders, are side tables of rosewood supported by carved dragons made in 1817 for the Banqueting room.

The furniture in the Chinese taste was, like the eighteenth century revival, marked by angularity, by a predilection for gay and tortuous forms, and for Chinese *motifs* such as the dragon and the pagoda, and by the introduction of Chinese figures. In the framework of chairs and light tables bamboo was frequently imitated; the surface of furniture was japanned and decorated in imitation of Chinese lacquer, and there are instances of the use of pseudo-Chinese inscriptions (Fig. 27).

Illustrations pp. 72-74.

[1] E. W. Brayley, *Illustrations of Her Majesty's Palace at Brighton*, 1838.
[2] Osbert Sitwell, *The Scarlet Tree*, 1946, p. 7.
[3] H. Clifford Smith, *Buckingham Palace* (Plate 271).

Materials and Processes

With the disuse of carving and inlay greater stress was laid upon the employment of dark lustrous cabinet woods, such as mahogany and kingwood, and woods of marked figure, such as calamander wood, zebrawood and amboyna.

In 'dressed apartments' East and West Indian satinwood was used, as well as rosewood and 'other varieties of woods brought from the East',[1] but the strong lemon colour of satinwood was relieved not by marquetry, but by inlay of ebony.[2] Mahogany remained in general use of drawing-room and library furniture.

'Rosewood' a trade term, which includes several species of wood, (*Dalbergia nigra* and *Dalbergia latifolia*) is heavy, dense, with dark streaks.

The great vogue for rosewood was to some extent due to the opening of a direct trade with Spanish America and the Portuguese territories of South America during the Napoleonic wars. Brazil, from which rosewood was imported, was one of the most important of these new markets. In Chambers' *Encyclopaedia* it is stated that lately 'much of the furniture even of a superior kind in Great Britain has often been stained of rosewood colour'.

The wood known to cabinet-makers as kingwood and highly prized by them from the late seventeenth century is the produce of a number of varieties of trees from South America, having timber of 'a rich violet grain, shading sometimes almost to black, and streaked with varying lighter and darker markings of golden yellow'.[3] It has a bright lustre, and a very smooth surface, and is finer in the grain than rosewood.

Amboyna is a name given to burr wood imported from the Moluccas (including Amboyna) and Borneo. The wood is brown in colour, tinged with yellow or reddish yellow, and is 'marked with little twisted curls and knots in a manner similar to, but more varied than, birds'-eye maple'.[4]

[1] Smith, *Household Furniture*, 1808, p. xiv.

[2] Bill of Samuel Beckwith. 'Two sattinwood shiffoniers ornamented with black lines inlaid.' For the drawing-room, Windsor Castle. Tradesmen's accounts, Lord Chamberlain's Office.

[3] Howard, *Manual of Timbers of the World* (ed. 1934), p. 247.

[4] *Ibid*. The second Duke of Northumberland (d. 1817) was sent by the King of Portugal some 'unsawed timber called amboyna wood', and from this tables, chairs and settees, formerly in the ante-drawing-room at Northumberland House, London, were made.

Materials and Processes

A considerable use was made of veneers with a striped or marbled figure for cabinets and small tables. Among these was calamander wood, imported from India and Ceylon, which shows bands and streaks of black and brown.[1] It is described as yielding veneers of unusual beauty, dark wavings and blotches, almost black, being gracefully disposed over a delicate fawn-coloured ground. Zebrawood, 'streaked with brown and white as the animal is, whence it has its name,'[2] has a similar effective figure, and has a firm hard texture, capable of a high polish, and was imported from Brazil. It was noticed as early as 1803 that supplies of this wood were scarce and by 1820 they were said to be exhausted.[3]

A lighter and cheaper grade of furniture was made from soft wood japanned with a variety of ground colours relieved by designs in contrasting colours or with *grisaille* picked out with gold. Some of this japanned furniture is found with its ground grained in imitation of the colour and figure of more costly woods. The taste for japanned[4] furniture was revived during the Chinese vogue.

The economic conditions after the French war, which 'doubled the cost and trebled the difficulty of genteel living', made it desirable for furniture to be plainer and less costly, and in the form of furniture, and in its technique, there were revolutionary changes. The curvature of fine furniture of the late eighteenth century meant expensive production, and in Regency furniture surfaces (except in the case of some animal legs of classic type) were straight. The difficult years of the Napoleonic Wars[5] probably caused the disappearance of inlaying which Sheraton, in his *Cabinet Dictionary* (1803), terms a 'very expensive mode' of decorating furniture. Carving was sparingly employed, and was often bronzed or gilt, a sign of the dominance of metal technique.

The craft of the carver in wood decayed rapidly in the early nineteenth century. There were only eleven master carvers in London and about sixty journeymen in the early nineteenth century. Many of the latter, we are told, 'are now very old; they make no shew of their work' and 'carving in wood has long been in the background

[1] Howard, *Manual of Timbers of the World* (ed. 1934), p. 157.

[2] Sheraton, *Cabinet Dictionary* (1803).

[3] Maria Edgworth noticed a table at Aston Hall in 1820 'of wood from Brazil, Zebrawood, and no more of it to be had for love or money'. *Life and Letters* (ed. A. J. C. Hare), Vol. I, p. 256.

[4] Japanning is 'here understood as the art of covering bodies by grounds of opake colours in varnish, which may be either afterwards decorated by paintings, or left in a plain state'—*The Artist's Assistant* (1801), p. 194.

[5] 'These costly times when Labour and materials . . . are so extravagantly dear'—D. Laing, *Hints for Dwellings* (1801), p. vii.

as a branch of the arts'.[1] An oblong panel of pearwood, dated 1807, in the corridor ante-chamber at Windsor Castle, is evidence of the skill of the unknown craftsman, who rivals Grinling Gibbons in the dexterity of his technique. It is executed entirely from one piece of pearwood, 'cut and undercut to the greatest depth and elaboration'.[2]

The Introduction of Wood-working Machinery

At the close of the eighteenth century, Sir Samuel Bentham within a few years invented and patented almost every known variety of woodworking machine. Bentham, who was for some years in Russia as a naval architect and engineer, invented shortly after 1779 'the first planing machine for wood that could really be called an organised operating machine',[3] and on his return to England in 1791 devised a large number of woodworking machines for use in convict prisons; and his brother Jeremy Bentham's house in Queen's Square, Westminster, was in 1791 converted into the first manufactory of woodcutting machines. 'In the Bentham factory were made machines for planing, moulding, rebating, grooving, mortising, sawing, in coarse and fine woods, in curved, winding and transverse directions —and shaping wood in all sorts of complicated forms.' In 1791 Samuel Bentham issued his patent for a planing machine, described by him as a 'method of planing divesting the operation of skill previously necessary and a reduction of brute force employed', the suggested motive power being wind, water, steam or animal strength. In 1793 Bentham, in an inclusive patent, originated 'practically every woodworking machine and process that is in use to-day'.

Metal Work

The casting of metals developed in the early nineteenth century, and in the words of the *Smelters' and Founders' Director* (1823), this branch of English manufacture was elevated 'far above that of any other country', and raised the articles which were formerly considered as merely 'gross and ponderous into the scale of ornamental embellishment'.

Composition ornament and painting was laid aside as less durable and less 'classic' than applications and inlays of metal. The French and English treatment of

[1] T. Martin, *The Circle of the Mechanical Arts*, p. 211.
[2] G. Laking, *Furniture at Windsor Castle*, p. 58.
[3] *Transactions of the American Society of Mechanical Engineers* (1929).

metal ornament at this date is distinct, the former specialising in applied chased ormolu mounts. On a few examples in the Royal Collection, from Deepdene, and at Southill (Figs. 3, 23) the applied mounts are elaborate, but in such cases a French 'bronzist' may have carried out Hope's and Holland's designs. The mounts on some rosewood bookcases made by Marsh and Tatham are unusually varied, and consist of paterae, entwined rods and the anthemium (Fig. 11).

George Smith mentions a Frenchman, Boileau,[1] as unsurpassed in his designs for casting in ormolu, and possessing 'a light airy and classic style'.[2]

The English speciality was an inlay of brass, which was not engraved, and contrasted with the ground of rosewood veneer 'without preventing it by any raised ornaments from being constantly rubbed'.[3] The ornaments, cut out of sheet brass in scroll and floral forms and classical patterns, were inserted into the veneer which was fretted to correspond, and the exactness of finish is admirable. Several drawings for inlay of this character are preserved in a portfolio in the Victoria and Albert Museum, dating from 1816.[4] The woods used as a ground were chosen for a dense, close-grained texture. The presence of this brass inlay on furniture is evidence of origin in London; for such metal work was a specialised trade, carried on in London in the neighbourhood of St. Martin's Lane and Long Acre. As this brass inlay had to be inserted during the progress of cabinet and chair making, it was difficult for country firms, at a distance from metal working centres, to compete in this form of enrichment with the London trade.

Brass colonnettes were also freely used as supports for galleries and shelves, and brass galleries finished the tops of sideboards, pedestals, secretaires and writing-tables.

The cast brass galleries of sideboards (such as Figs. 163-164), are noticeable. Cast metal fittings such as paw feet and handles, are illustrated in catalogues of metal working firms. A tendency to overload furniture with brass is noticed in 1820 as 'frequently seen';[5] and inlay of intricate design appears during the second quarter of the nineteenth century.

---

[1] See Records of Furniture-makers.   [2] *Cabinet Makers' and Upholsterers' Guide* (1826).

[3] Hope, *Household Furniture*, 1807, p. 35.

[4] One is inscribed 'for Mr. Boulton's oak cabinet, 1816'; another for 'a sofa table'. *Album of Miscellaneous Sketches*, Print and Engravings Department, Victoria and Albert Museum.

[5] 'There is another very important part in designing furniture in which the cabinet-maker ought to be skilful, that is harmonising metals with woods, so as not to overload the articles with bronze, or ormolu, which is so frequently seen.'—R. Brown, *Rudiments of Drawing Cabinet Furniture*, 1820, p. x.

Instances of this are the set of amboyna tables made in 1816 (Fig. 96), and a grand piano of walnut made for the Prince Regent about 1818, in which the sides of the case, and the pedestal support are enriched with large panels of brass inlay.[1]

Sheraton notices metal cockheads on mouldings as an innovation, and as 'a substantial though an expensive method of working'.[2] An imitation of Boulle, an inlay of metal and tortoiseshell, was made in England during the Regency, at the Buhl factory, in Queen Street, Edgeware Road, which was owned by a Frenchman, Le Gaigneur, and Thomas Parker, of Air Street, also manufactured 'Buhl furniture'. In the golden drawing-room, Carlton House, two circular tables are shown in Pyne's *Royal Residences* 'of Buhl, executed in Rosewood, tortoiseshell and ormolu'.[3]

Polish

The preference for smooth glass-like surfaces led to the adoption of 'French' polish, a composition said to have been brought to this country after the peace of 1814, when much furniture was unfortunately stripped and repolished. For this the polish, which consists of shellac, is dissolved in spirits of wine or methylated spirits and is applied with a rubber with a continuous circular motion, without allowing the rubber to rest.[4]

[1] Illustrated in H. Clifford Smith, *Buckingham Palace*, Fig. 165.   [2] *Cabinet Dictionary* (1803), p. 257.

[3] *Royal Residences* (1819), Vol. III, plate 60.

[4] The original 'French' polishing was different from the present—a much better quality of spirit was used: the grain of the wood was oiled and then filled in carefully with fine powdered pumice and spirit and very highly polished in this state; the 'French' polish (which was shellac and spirit) was applied after. No 'stain' in the polish was then used. To-day 'French' polishing is a much quicker process and the result is very different.

Seat Furniture & Stools

Sydney Smith, in reviewing the *Household Furniture* of Thomas Hope, pointed out that it is a 'substantial part' of the convenience of chairs and tables to be easily moved, and that they had become progressively lighter and lighter for the great part of the eighteenth century.[1] The cane-seated seats of painted beech which were in fashion in the late years of the eighteenth century are the lightest phase in this long evolution. In Regency seat furniture the new severity finds expression in the reeding of members, the classic character of the painted decoration, and the emphasis upon horizontality in the treatment of the back.

The variety of design in seat furniture is a feature of this period, and by 1820 it was said that it 'now baffles the most skilful artists to produce any new forms'.[2]

The lion-leg and the lion-monopodium are figured in Sheraton's *Cabinet Dictionary* and appear in certain examples (Figs. 34, 35). During the early nineteenth century there was a revival of the lyre *motif* for the splat (Fig. 69), and in a contemporary account of an American private yacht (named *Cleopatra's Barge*) in 1817, the sofas in the saloon are described as having backs shaped like an ancient lyre'.[3]

A distinction was drawn between seat-furniture made of mahogany or satinwood, and what were termed 'fancy' seat-furniture which were made of beech painted or japanned. An American advertisement by William Challen, in 1797 Fancy Chair Maker from London,[4] states that he manufactures 'all sorts of dyed japanned and bamboo chairs, settees, etc., every article in the fancy chair line executed in the newest and most approved London patterns'. A variety of fancy seat-furniture was the bamboo, in which the beech framework, turned and shaped and painted in imitation of bamboo, was considered suitable for 'rooms slightly decorated'.[5] The imitation of the bamboo, 'a kind of Indian reed', by turning beech

[1] *Edinburgh Review* (1807), Vol. X, p. 483.

[2] R. Brown, *Rudiments of Drawing Cabinet Furniture* (1820), p. 25.

[3] *Salem Gazette*, January, 1817. A contemporary account of the yacht, quoted by G. Singleton, *Furniture of Our Forefathers*, p. 555, describes them in fuller detail. 'The sofas in the cabin were of mahogany and birds'-eye maple, and measured eleven feet in length. The lyres forming the back were strung with thick brass wire'.

[4] Quoted in Singleton, *Furniture of Our Forefathers*, p. 640.

[5] George Smith, *Household Furniture* (1808), p. 16.

into the same form, and painting them to match the colour of the reeds or cane is described by Sheraton in his *Cabinet Dictionary*.[1] An account of Elward Marsh and Tatham in 1802 includes 'bamboo chairs japanned and Indian bamboo tables' for the Royal Pavilion at Brighton.[2]

In the last decade of the eighteenth century the designs of chairs follow with slight modification the traditional form (Figs. 30-33). The arms of these arm-chairs are set high in the back uprights, and in most instances are swept up to these near the top, giving a characteristic high-shouldered appearance. Sometimes arm-supports rise from the side-rails, but in the majority they are continuations of the legs. In one design, the arm curves downward in an arc, touching the seat frame and finishing in a small scroll; and in another the arm is extended in a scroll over the concave arm-support.

A revolutionary change in design was the copying of the Greek chair of the fourth and fifth centuries, which was also copied in Rome. In this chair (κλισμός) the back and rear legs formed a continuous curve, which the front legs bend forward to balance. The back uprights which are crossed at shoulder height by a board, swing forward in profile, as in the stela of Hegiso in the museum, Athens.

A bronze cross-framed seat, drawn by Charles Heathcote Tatham from the original in Rome in 1800, is figured in his *Etchings of Ancient Ornamental Architecture*,[3] and close adaptations of this appear in Hope's *Household Furniture*[4] and in George Smith's publication in the following year.

In the case of chairs, legs, composed of double reversed curves, crossed in the centre, were also introduced. Two arrangements of supports occur, one with the curved legs on both sides joined by a turned stretcher, and the other with curved legs at the front and straight legs at the back. A set of chairs, with only the curved front legs crossing, was made in 1828 by Morel and Seddon for Windsor Castle.

In the type described as reading or conversation chairs, the back is tapered to a narrow waist to allow the occupant to sit astride facing the back. The top rail is flat, to serve as a rest, and in the case of reading chairs is fitted with folding candle brackets.

Varieties of arm-chairs which are figured in Sheraton's *Cabinet Dictionary*

---

[1] *Cabinet Dictionary* (1803), p. 29.

[2] Quoted in H. Clifford Smith, *Buckingham Palace*, p. 112.   [3] 1803 edition, Plate 75.

[4] Described as 'antique seats from bronze originals at Rome'. Plate 20, described in the text as 'an armchair after the manner of the ancient curule chairs'.

include a tub-shaped chair, an upholstered *fauteuil* with moulded top rail and arms, and a *bergère* with caned back and arms.[1]

Arc-backed armchairs, derived partly from the marble throne, and partly from the French *bergère*, are illustrated in Hope's *Household Furniture*. At Buckingham Palace is a set of six *bergères* of this type, caned up to the wide scrolled and upholstered top rail. These were made by Morel and Hughes in 1812, and described in the Royal accounts as 'large elegant *bergère* chairs, carved chimeras'.

The design of a pair of throne-chairs for use at Royal Councils at Carlton House is based on a Roman type; and one of these (placed by the council table) is clearly shown in a plate in *Royal Residences*.[2] The backs are carried to the ground and are carved with acanthus scrolls and foliations, and the side supports are winged sphinxes whose wings form the elbows of the chair (Fig. 29).

An armchair having a back with a pronounced rake is illustrated in George Smith's *Household Furniture* where it is described as being of French invention, and illustrated in profile to show the curvature.

Settees, Sofas (Couches)

The sofa and the settee are distinct articles of furniture, the settee being an extension of the armchair, while the sofa or couch was a development of the day-bed and was adapted for reclining.[3] The classic couch dominated the design of the Regency and of the contemporary French Empire. When Madame Recamier was painted by David in 1800, the couch on which she is shown seated is of classic type, resting on supports consisting of many-membered turnings.[4] In a design by Sheraton, a 'Grecian couch' has a head, and a low foot-piece. In the inventory of Southill taken in 1815, the couch (Fig. 67) is described as 'a single-head couch'.

The legs were either short and top-shaped, outward curved, or in the form of lion feet.

Sheraton[5] recommends the furnishing of a drawing-room with two sofas, to be covered with figured silk or satin, and to have 'cushions to fit their backs, together with bolsters at each end', and sets of two sofas are to be found at Southill. In the drawing-room illustrated and described by George Smith, four sofas are grouped

[1] Sometimes the seats are caned, having loose cushions.—*Cabinet Dictionary*, p. 19 and Plate 8.

[2] *Royal Residences* (1819), Vol. III, plate 25.

[3] Sofa; a long stuffed seat with a back and end; used for reclining.—*New English Dictionary*.

[4] Portrait of Madame Recamier (1800) in the Louvre.   [5] *Drawing Book* (1791–4).

round a centre table; and they are described in Ackermann's *Repository* (1809) as 'an indispensable piece of furniture in a library'. They are hinted at as a relaxation after an exhausting day in *Mansfield Park*, when the guests at a picnic in the grounds of Sotherton 'returned to the house together there to lounge away the time as they could with sofas and chitchat'. In modest households its use by the younger members of the family was resented by their elders, and Mrs. Norris, in Jane Austen's *Mansfield Park*, complains that it is 'a shocking trick for a young person to be always lolling on a sofa'. There would often be but one in the house; and in less luxurious households, to lie down, or even to lean back, was a luxury permitted only to old persons and invalids. Sofas are instanced by Cobbett among the innovations that accompanied the increased wealth of the tenant farmer, who was able to afford a fox-hunting horse and polished boots, as well as a house 'crammed up with sofas, pianos, and all sorts of fooleries'. The vogue for sofas is shown by the large proportion of these to chairs in a set of seat-furniture (made for Windsor Castle in 1828) which consists of four large sofas, four small sofas, ten arm chairs and fifteen chairs.

The fantastic sofa in the form of a crocodile (Fig. 20), which is described in an inventory of 1820 as 'an antique or Grecian couch with crocodile legs',[1] preserves its original bluish-green colouring, with flutings and mouldings picked out in gold.

The Ottoman

The ottoman (or Turkey sofa), a long and low upholstered seat,[2] without back or ends, is described by Sheraton as a fashionable novelty in 'imitation of the Turkish mode of sitting', and is shown by him in his illustration of the Chinese Room at Carlton House, as extending the whole width of the room. George Smith defines it as a long couch, which should be placed on the chimney side of the room with similar seats on the opposite side.

Window Stools, Stools and Footstools

The small window benches or stools which were set in window recesses are closely related to designs for chairs, their ends being reduced replicas of chair backs. Stools serving as 'ornamental centre seats in elegant rooms' continued to be made as adjuncts to large sets of seat furniture for state rooms.

Among novel features in the design of footstools is the appearance of scrolled

[1] *Country Life*, May 10, 1930.

[2] 'The modern ottoman may be more elegant than the old sofa, but an old and infirm person is very apt to tumble backwards from it.'—*Anecdotes and Egotisms of Henry Mackenzie* (1745–1831), ed. 1927, p. 14.

ends, rising above the upholstered surface, giving the piece the appearance of a miniature couch (Fig. 82); a type figured in George Smith's *Household Furniture*. In another design the anthemium is applied to the four angles (Fig. 7). A stool in the form of a S-shaped scroll, covered on the upper face, is also figured in Ackermann's *Repository*.

Caning was much employed for the seats and backs, and in the *Cabinet Dictionary* (1803) Sheraton writes that about thirty years ago it had gone out of fashion, but that 'on the revival of japanning furniture, it began to be brought gradually into use, and to a state of improvement'.

Illustrations pp. 75-101.

Tables

Tables, structurally, fall into three types; the first supported by legs at the corners; the second, supported on a central pillar or pedestal; the third, supported at ends.

'Classical' Tables

A table with round top and supported by a central shaft, or by three animal legs, was revived (Figs. 101-102). Another type of table is supported by a splayed central support. A table of this form (Fig. 16)[1], with its top and splayed support inlaid with ebony and silver, was made for Thomas Hope, and figures in his *Household Furniture*.

Side tables are given prominence in the *Drawing Book* (1791-1794), and their tops were (as Sheraton notes), sometimes of solid marble. The use of marble slabs was carried on into the nineteenth century, when the design of many of these tables incorporated lion monopodia, or Egyptian terminal figures. A looking-glass plate was often placed at the back for the sake of the reflection (Fig. 92 and 103). The pair of pier tables from Southill are shelved for china. Examples of the finished classical furniture of this period are the pier tables at Windsor Castle,[2] each surmounted by a slab of verde-antique marble and supported at either end by seated gryphons, which were made originally for Carlton House.

Dining Tables

During the second half of the eighteenth century, large dining tables were built up of units and described as a 'set of dining tables'. These units consisted of two end tables, each with four fixed legs and D-shaped, rectangular or semi-circular top, and a central unit with rectangular flaps supported on gate-legs. The flaps were attached to each other by means of brass clips and sockets. Such tables are rarely met with complete, as their component sections have often been separated, and regarded as side or smaller dining tables. In a letter written in 1800, Jane Austen writes of one of these composite tables that had just arrived: 'The two ends put together form one constant table for everything, and the centre piece stands

[1] In the Victoria and Albert Museum W-13, 1936.   [2] G. Laking, *Furniture at Windsor Castle*, Plate 23.

exceedingly well under the glass and holds a great deal most commodiously.'[1] Some very large composite tables were made, and in Gillow's Cost books for 1795 is a sketch of a table in ten sections, measuring twenty-four feet in length. In Gillow's Cost books from 1784 to 1800, the supports were four tapered legs to each section. A variant support was a central pillar, supported by four 'claws', and in Sheraton's illustration of the dining parlour at Carlton House there is shown 'a long range of dining tables, standing on pillars with four claws each, which is now the fashionable way of making these tables'.[2]

In the year 1800 a patent was taken out for extending tables by Richard Gillow. His improvement (known as the patent table) consisted in 'attaching to a table mounted upon a frame or legs, or a pillar and claws, wooden or metal sliders (which run in dovetail, T or square or cylindrical or other grooves) with or without wheels or rollers'.[3] These sliders are drawn out to the length required and flaps are laid upon them.

In another form of extending table, the moveable part, when drawn out, forms a lazy tongs, and the legs, of which there are two to each division of the tongs, are fixed in joints made of brass, iron or any other suitable material.[4]

In the case of extending round tables with a central support, shaped sections are added forming an outer border, fixed by long bearers and kept rigid by brackets. Sometimes an additional outer section is added. A later expanding table is constructed so that 'the sections composing its surface may be caused to diverge from a common centre, and that the spaces caused thereby may be filled up by inserting leaves or 'filling' pieces. 'The expansion may be by hand or by turning the surface and bed of the table round the pillar'.[5]

The heavier supports characteristic of the second decade of the nineteenth century are shown in the dining-table from Liverpool Town Hall, in which the bases of the stout columns are carved with acanthus. By 1835 an 'excessive breadth' was fashionable, for 'the purpose of holding first the cumbrous ornaments and lights, secondly in some cases the dessert, at the same time with the side dishes'.[6]

The round dining-table was revived in the first years of the nineteenth century. A visitor to Cobham Hall in 1804 observed that 'they dine at a round table, Lord Darnley sometimes sitting in one part and sometimes in another, and Lady

[1] Austen Leigh, *A Memoir of Jane Austen*, p. 58. [2] *Cabinetmakers' and Upholsterers' Drawing-book*, p. 440.
[3] *Abridgements of Specifications*, Vol. 39. [4] George Remington's patent, Dec. 1807.
[5] Robert Jupe's patent, March, 1835. [6] The *Original*, Sept. 2, 1835.

Darnley always on his right hand'.[1] The advantage of the circular form was, we are told,[2] 'to avoid distinction in guests.' The round table in Jane Austen's novel *Emma* (published in 1816), is described as the 'modern' table which had superseded the Pembroke, "upon which all Mr. Woodhouse's meals had been crowded."

Pembroke and Sofa Tables

The flap table described as a 'Pembroke', having flaps supported on hinged wooden brackets, was widely used early in the reign of George III[3] and continued in fashion during the Regency. In Jane Austen's unfinished fragment, *The Watsons*, the Pembroke serves as a tea-table.

A longer table, the sofa-table, was also constructed with fly brackets, and Sheraton describes such tables as 'used before a sofa and generally made between five and six feet long and from twenty-two inches by two feet broad. Ladies' (it is added) 'chiefly occupy them to draw, write or read upon'. The junction of the flap and centre section in these tables is rule-jointed, and there is a drawer or drawers in the frieze'

A variety of patterns was employed for the supports, ranging from end-supports (Figs. 95, 97, 99-100) and a pedestal (or balusters) resting on a platform supported by splayed legs, as in the examples made in the second decade of the nineteenth century (Fig. 96 and Fig. 98).

Occasional Tables, Nests of Tables

'Little tables placed in every direction' were counted among the modern and confusing additions to an old-fashioned parlour in Jane Austen's *Persuasion*,[4] and there exist many small portable tables which were used to set about the rooms to hold lights, needlework or papers. 'I think no room looks really comfortable or even quite furnished (writes Fanny Burney) without two tables, one to keep the wall, the other to stand here, there and everywhere, and hold letters and *make the agreeable*.'[5]

Small oblong tables of rosewood, satinwood and mahogany supported at either end by columnar legs resting on splayed feet are frequent in the early nineteenth century. Two tables from Southill have end-supports; one, a lady's writing-table of

[1] The *Farington Diary*, March, 1804.   [2] Ackermann's *Repository*, 1827 (Vol. 36).

[3] A Pembroke table of mahogany was supplied by Thomas Chippendale to Nostell Priory on 24th June, 1766. The earliest use of the word given in the *New English Dictionary* appears in 1778.

[4] Finished in 1816 and published in 1818.

[5] Letter of Fanny Burney, Sept. 6, 1801, quoted in Constance Hill's *Juniper Hall*, p. 258.

rosewood, has wide applegreen panels in the centre of each support mounted with ormolu. The Greek detail of the scrolled feet is carved and gilt (Fig. 2). In a second table (Fig. 1) the top is mounted with a panel of mosaic in hard stones—lapis lazuli, malachite and onyx, and the columnar rosewood legs are mounted with ormolu upright leaves and reeding; and the feet are also ormolu-mounted. A number of small tables are of tripod form; a small monopodium at Southill, one of a pair, has as its centre support a reeded column springing from a lotus-calyx (Fig. 114).

Nests of four tables of graduated size, which are illustrated in Sheraton's *Cabinet Dictionary*, were known as 'quartetto tables',[1] and defined as 'a kind of small table made to draw out of each other and again enclosed within each other when not in use' (Figs. 116, 117).[2]

Work Tables

The work table differs from the small occasional table in having a lifting top disclosing a well or small drawers. In many of these a bag or pouch is affixed to a sliding frame. The pouch table is defined by Sheraton[3] as 'a table with a bag used by ladies to work at, in which bag they deposit their fancy needlework. The work bags . . . are suspended to a frame which draws forward.'

A work table formed as a globe on a stand was among the innovations of the period. A work table of this form, having the quarters of the globe divided by fine holly lines meeting at the top in a brass patera, is in the Lady Lever Museum.[4] When open it discloses a small temple backed by looking-glass, and fitted with columns and parquet flooring, and having numerous small drawers and receptacles for work. The legs supporting the globe are united by a galleried bowl to contain the odds and ends of needlework. A second table of this form, in the Royal collection is inlaid with the signs of the Zodiac (Figs. 120-121).

A combined games and work table was in use in the early nineteenth century, which has the reversible top or a slide inlaid with a chess or backgammon board (Fig. 119).

Games Tables

Fewer card-tables appear to have been made in the Regency period, but there was a revival of the combined games and card table. This type has a centre

---

[1] *Quartetto* = quartet, a set of four things.   [2] *Cabinet Dictionary*, p. 293.
[3] *Cabinet Dictionary*, p. 292.   [4] *Catalogue of the Lever Art Gallery and Museum*, Plate 89.

with lifting top, having a backgammon-board on one side and a draught-board on the other. A popular game of cards was 'Loo',[1] and a table made in 1810 for Papworth Hall is described in George Oakley's account as 'a calamanderwood circular loo table upon pedestal and claws, the top inlaid with a border of stars in brass and ebony'.

Illustrations pp. 102-119.

[1] A round game popular in the last years of the eighteenth and early nineteenth century. In Charlotte Smith's *Ethelinda* (1789), Vol. II, p. 132: 'Dinner was no sooner over than the loo table was introduced into the drawing-room'.

Library & Writing Tables

The accepted type of kneehole pedestal writing-table, a table with a central kneehole flanked by tiers of drawers, gave little scope for variation except in detail, but the lion support and *motifs* from the Egyptian style are introduced in the early nineteenth century. In the pedestal writing-table made in 1805 for Stourhead by the younger Thomas Chippendale, the round ends are supported by what the maker describes as 'therms with Egyptian heads', while the engaged terms flanking the pedestals finish in classical heads (Fig. 127).

Examples of classical treatment are a pedestal table (Fig. 125) with its panelled doors mounted with bronze reliefs of the Athenian owl, and Greek characters within a laurel wreath and frieze inlaid with a Greek fret in brass on an ebony ground; and a table in the Victoria and Albert Museum which has its cupboards flanked by caryatid terms, and frieze, sides and panels carved in low relief with classical *motifs* (Fig. 126).

The Carlton House table bore this name very soon after its introduction, but there is no evidence in the Royal accounts that it was made for the Prince of Wales's London house. It is a table with drawers in the frieze and a superstructure extending round the sides and back and fitted with small drawers and cupboards. A sketch of a 'Carleton House table' appears in Gillow's Cost books for 1796. The superstructure is stepped at each side, and this design is repeated in the cost books two years later (1798) for the Earl of Derby. In several examples the sides are carried up to the level of the back. The first suggestion of the Carlton House type is a design in Sheraton's Appendix to his *Drawing Book* (1793) described as a 'Lady's Drawing and Writing table', differing only from the usual pattern in having a rising desk in the middle to slide forward (Fig. 234). A variant is the example from Hinchingbrooke, with its superstructure of even height (Fig. 21). In some Carlton House tables (Figs. 128-129) the legs have a tassel capping similar to a rosewood writing-table at Buckingham Palace daiing from about 1813.

Tambour and cylinder fronted writing-tables continued to be made. A tambour writing-table from Southill (Fig. 9) is veneered with rosewood and surmounted by a white marble top. The brackets between the legs and the under framing and the capping on the legs are of ormolu. A cylindrical writing-table, resting on end supports with splayed feet is illustrated in the *Cabinet Dictionary* (Fig. 232). A slightly different pattern is a knee-hole writing desk, in which the lower part is boat-shaped.

A new pattern was the table with revolving circular top in which the deep frieze is fitted with drawers. This pattern appears in Gillow's Cost books in 1795, and is described as 'a round mahogany library table' (Fig. 231). As the top revolved, each drawer could be brought in front of the writer. The centre support ranges from the pillar and claw to the massive column resting on a flat base. In a composite piece (Fig. 141), the base of the table is shelved and protected by a trellis of brass wire.

The Davenport

The earliest use of the term Davenport for a small ornamental writing-table or escritoire fitted with drawers[1] is given in the *New English Dictionary* in 1853, but examples of the pattern (a small case of drawers surmounted by a desk) exist dating from the early nineteenth century.

Illustrations pp. 120-129.

---

[1] *Practical Mechanics*, Journal VI, p. 212. 'This very elegant and convenient desk is similar to an ordinary Davenport'.

Bookcases & Bookshelves

There are references to increased demand for bookcases in the early nineteenth century, and to their manufacture by cabinet-makers[1] ('who felt an interest in the increase of books') as 'the leading article of employ'. The bookcase in two stages remained essentially the same. An interesting variant in the Royal Collection has an advanced lower stage surmounted by a white marble slab, and this feature and the quality of the ormolu mounts applied to the frieze and pilasters give it a French air (Fig. 11). In many cases, the bookcase was subjected in its proportions and decorations to Greek canons, and is crowned by a 'Greek' pediment and antefixae.

The bookcase designed by Thomas Hope for Deepdene (Fig. 14) is an instance of Egyptian massiveness. Each of the cupboard doors of the upper stage are glazed with a single sheet of glass and divided by pilasters headed by carved Egyptian sphinx-heads, while the projecting base of the upper stage is supported by four 'lion monopodia'. A bookcase of mahogany inlaid with ebony, also in two stages, which was made by George Oakley in 1810 for Papworth Hall, is described by its maker as a 'mahogany winged library case in the Grecian style, the doors fitted with brass trellis wire and quilled silk curtains with best locks and keys'. At either end of the slightly projecting wings are antefixae, and the recessed centre is covered by a small pediment, to which is applied a small-scale enrichment in gilt brass. Dwarf bookcases, movable bookstands and revolving bookcases supplemented and to some extent ousted, the two-storied type.

Bookcases were affected in their proportions by what George Smith terms the 'lowness adopted in the present design'[2] in order to leave the walls free for paintings. He illustrates dwarf bookcases, consisting of two pedestal ends and three low compartments, in which the centre is occupied by small books. Such dwarf bookcases were usually made in pairs, and in some instances were surmounted by a marble slab. The doors were glazed or protected by a trellis or mesh of brass wire. Dwarf bookcases were designed by Holland for the piers between the windows in the golden drawing-room at Carlton House. These were surmounted by a marble slab,

[1] Sheraton, *Cabinet Dictionary* (1803), pp. 70–1.   [2] *A Collection of Designs for Household Furniture* (1808), p. 10.

and mounted with 'angle pillars of palm trees in ormolu'.[1] A type intermediate between a low bookcase and a commode was designed by Holland for Southill. In a sketchbook of his in the library of the Royal Institute of British Architects there is a drawing for 'the bookcase tables for the piers in the library'. Flanking the shelved centre are concave panels decorated with a Greek detail.

Many low and light bookcases were designed 'calculated to contain all the books that may be desired for a sitting-room without reference to the library'.[2] The type with receding shelves (Figs. 145, 149) and fitted with casters appears in Gillow's Cost book in 1799 as a 'moving library', and this term also appears in the *Cabinet Dictionary*.[3]

A novelty was the circular bookcase or bookstand in which shelves revolve round a central column (Figs. 158, 159). A patent was taken out in July 1808 by Benjamin Crosby for 'a machine or stand for books, which may be made either circular, square or any other convenient shape, and which may be turned or moved at pleasure; with cases to receive books'. It is composed of a central shaft or column and fixed shelves at suitable distances above each other containing each a roller or cylinder and screwed to the shaft. A bookshelf is fixed to each cylinder. Each bookshelf is divided into compartments by cross pieces, the interstices being filled up with 'labels and popular books, or in any other ornamental way'.

This type is illustrated in Ackermann's *Repository* (March, 1810) as an 'ingenious contrivance'. The projector (according to the note accompanying the plate) 'seems to have had in recollection the conveniences afforded by the set of circular and movable tables formerly known by the appellation of dumb waiters'. A cylindrical pedestal, formed of two shelves as a base, supports the upper and movable part, which consists of shelves progressively diminishing in diameter. 'Each shelf is furnished with a corresponding shelf at a distance above it, and the two shelves thus situated are moved horizontally about an upright centre which passes through the whole machine.' The pedestal is furnished with substantial feet and rollers, so that the piece can be wheeled to different parts of a room, or from one room to another. 'This bookcase', the note continues, 'appears to afford some valuable conveniences, as, for instance, it may be placed in a recess, or corner of a room in which from local circumstances it might be inconvenient or impossible to dispose the same number of books'. In some cases, dummy books divide the shelves, and in the design in the *Repository* there is a turned wooden urn finial.

[1] Pyne, *Royal Residences*, Vol. III, p. 58. [2] Ackermann's *Repository* (1823).

[3] The tea-room or breakfast-room may abound with . . . moving libraries.'—*Cabinet Dictionary*, (p. 219).

Bookcases & Bookshelves

Secretaires

Secretaires have, like bookcases, a glazed and shelved upper stage or cabinet, but are fitted with a writing drawer in the lower stage.

Bookshelves

The small open bookshelves of mahogany or satinwood, which supplemented the bookcase, differed from their eighteenth century hanging shelves in the structure of their sides, which were of brass wire, instead of perforated wood. This substitute of wire for wooden ends 'lightened the shelves, so that 'they could be moved by a lady to any sitting room'. A feature of both cupboards and bookcases of the Regency is the open shelved structure which often surmounts them.

Library steps, which are defined in the *Cabinet Dictionary*[1] as steps placed 'in a library for the use of raising a person so as to reach any book', were an essential part of the furniture of large libraries, and were often contrived to fold up into the upper part of a stool or table. Several examples of these contrivances are illustrated in the *Dictionary of English Furniture*, Vol. II. Library steps were described in a survey of Alnwick in 1785, where one of a pair of tables was 'by an ingenious device opened and forms a pair of commodious steps for reaching any of the Books from the higher shelves'. The two examples of library steps illustrated in the Appendix to Sheraton's *Drawing Book* were, he writes, taken 'from steps made by Mr. Campbell, upholsterer to the Prince of Wales', and were first made for George III. In one design 'the table when enclosed, serves as a library table and has a rising flap, supported by a base, to write on'. In the second, and simple design, the upper flight of steps folds down upon the under flight, and both rise up and slide into the frieze, which is afterwards closed by a flap, which has the appearance of a drawer front. The resting post at the top also folds down to the side of the steps.

In 1811, Morgan and Saunders showed a design in Ackermann's *Repository* for a metamorphic library chair, in which 'an elegant and comfortable library chair' is combined with a set of steps. As may be seen from the illustration of the contrivance in the Library of Trinity College, Oxford, the chair is converted into steps by turning the back of the chair downwards. The contrivance 'corresponds so closely with the design as to leave no doubt of its origin. After one hundred and twenty years it still justifies the makers' claim that it is firm, safe and solid as a rock' (Figs. 161-162).[2]

Illustrations pp. 130-142.

[1] 1803.　　　[2] Described and illustrated, *Country Life*, September 20, 1930.

Sideboards, Dining & Drinking Accessories

The sideboard table without drawers flanked by pedestals[1] carrying vases or knife boxes, a development of the type designed by Robert Adam, continued to be made. In the inventory of furniture at Papworth Hall (in 1810) there is an entry of a 'capital mahogany sideboard supported on a stand, reeded legs and carved and bronzed paw feet with antique bronze heads', and pedestals to match.[2] The sideboard fitted with pedestal cupboard developed into a massive piece of furniture with a considerable storage-capacity. A sideboard formerly in Nelson's cabin in the *Victory*, and dating from about 1800, is of this massive type,[3] having deep pedestal ends, each fitted with a drawer and a cupboard, a projecting centre, and panelled back-piece, rising above the top of the sideboard. Such pedestals, prolonged almost to the floor and often rising above the level of the centre, were fitted with a drawer at the top which supplied the place of a knife-vase or box. A rosewood sideboard dating from about 1815–1820, in the Victoria and Albert Museum, shows the late features of projecting central shelf with a scrolled back-piece, flanked by two tapering pedestals, each fitted with two drawers. Each pedestal supports a tapering rectangular knife-box with a hinged lid and feet in the form of brass balls.[4]

Dining and Drinking Accessories (Wine Tables, Dumb Waiters)

As prolonged drinking after dinner was still a polite custom, specialised wine or 'social' tables were produced in the second half of the eighteenth century. A gentleman's social table, figured in the *Cabinet Maker's Book of Prices* for 1793, shows a kidney-shaped table for the sitters, combined with a smaller table, in which the

---

[1] Pedestals were 'designed for holding plates for dinner and contained racks and a heater', according to Sheraton, *Cabinet Dictionary* (1803). In Smith's *Designs for Household Furniture* (1808), one pedestal is fitted as a plate-warmer, while the other contains a tray capable of holding six or eight bottles.

[2] MS. inventory of furniture supplied by Oakley for Papworth Hall, 1810.

[3] Exhibited on loan in the forecabin of the *Victory*, 1928.   [4] W. 149, 1923.

drum consists of a 'cylinder of tin or copper, and a mahogany top fitted into the cylinder, and cut to receive five tin bottle-cases'. A horseshoe-shaped drinking table, fitted with two japanned ice-pails, is figured in Gillow's Cost books (July, 1801), where it is described as a 'social table'.[1] In an example from the London Museum, the bottles were contained in two metal coasters, hinged to a brass rod. In some examples, adjustable circular fans are fitted to the table to serve as fire-screens.

The dumb waiter of the Regency period, defined in the *Cabinet Dictionary* (1803) as a 'useful piece of furniture to serve in some respects the place of a waiter', differs from the earlier patterns in the form of its tripod (Figs. 175-176).

Plate and Cutlery Stands (*Canterburies*)

Among the convenient accessories introduced into the dining-room in the late eighteenth century were stands for carrying plates, and larger stands partitioned into spaces for cutlery and plates (Figs. 177-178). Sheraton defines these 'supper Canterburies' as a supper tray 'made to stand by a table at supper, with a circular end, and three divisions cross-wise, to hold knives, forks, and plates at that end, which is made circular on purpose';[2] and illustrates two designs, one having a circular top and a platform fitted with small divisions; the other having a tray top; a platform divided into partitions for knives, forks, etc.

Illustrations pp. 143-152.

[1] An early reference to a specialised drinking table is at Howth Castle (1746–1752), where a 'round mahogany drinking-table appears in the dining parlour'.—Ball, *The House of Howth*, p. 164.

[2] *Cabinet Dictionary* (1803), p. 127.

Pedestals, The What-not, Canterburies & Fire-screens

Pedestals for lamps, candelabra, vases or busts were characteristic of the period, and the form was adapted for the display of classical ornament. In George Smith's *Household Furniture*, they are recommended for a number of purposes and situations.[1] 'In galleries for pictures or antiquities these supports are appropriate for busts or statues; they are equally useful in halls or staircases and need not be rejected in drawing-rooms.' In the latter place, they served to carry vases or figures carrying branches for lights.

Four candelabra of gilt wood, made for the Prince Regent in 1811[2] are based on the Roman type of candelabrum. The triangular base is surmounted by three seated lions supporting a column surmounted by ormolu branches for lights.

The What-not

This open stand, fitted with tiers of shelves, is not illustrated in trade-catalogues of the late eighteenth century, and is first mentioned in the year 1808.[3] It is defined in the *New English Dictionary* as 'an open stand with shelves one above another for keeping or displaying various objects, as ornaments, curiosities, books, papers, etc'. An early evidence of this type is the rosewood examples fitted with shelves, and mounted with ormolu (Fig. 180).

Stands to hold music and portfolios for the numerous engravings published at this time also became recognised as necessary pieces of furniture.

Canterburies

Under this term music stands are defined by Sheraton in his *Dictionary* as 'made with two or three hollow-topped partitions', resting on legs fitted with casters and 'adapted to run in under a pianoforte'. In the rosewood canterbury (Fig. 182)

[1] *Designs for Household Furniture* (1808).

[2] By Tatham, Bailey & Saunders. Illustrated in H. Clifford Smith, *Buckingham Palace*, Figs. 159.

[3] 'The old chairs, tables, what-nots and sofas.'—Sarah, Lady Lyttleton, *Correspondence* (1808) (ed. 1902), p. 54.

with sides fitted with wire trellis-work, to hold the bound music-books and port-folios, there is a drawer beneath to hold unbound music.

Fire-screens

The fire-screen was an article of general use, and 'admitted of every species of decoration according to the character of the room'.[1] An attempt to give a classical impress to furniture is evident in the pole-screen illustrated in Hope's *Household Furniture*. A pair of rosewood pole-screens with carved and gilt enrichments, carrying a brass pole with a lance-shaped terminal bearing a shield-shaped shield of rosewood carved with a classical thunderbolt were designed for Thomas Hope and were formerly at Deepdene. A distinctive feature of the pole-screens of the last years of the eighteenth and early nineteenth century is the solid base or block upon which the pole rests.

About this time the banner-screen, in which an unframed piece of stuff hung from a transverse rod, became popular.

In the pole-screen (Fig. 185) the tripod base persists, in the form of animal supports, which are carved and gilt. The slender rod has a carved and gilt base and the panel is painted with an arabesque in water colours by Delabriese, the French artist who painted the walls of the boudoir at Southill. The framed panels were usually painted or worked in a design such as 'the taste of the amateur may suggest'.[2]

Illustrations pp. 153-155.

[1] *Household Furniture*, 1808.   [2] Ackermann's *Repository* (1815).

Commodes & Chiffoniers

I t proved impossible to translate the eighteenth-century commode, which depended so largely upon its subtlety of shaping and its surface decoration of marquetry and painting, into the new classical idiom. Commodes 'intended for the drawing-rooms and also for living-rooms, [having] therefore doors to screen or secure such articles as may be placed in them' are illustrated in George Smith's *Household Furniture* (1808), and described as being made of 'rosewood, satinwood, or in gold on a white ground, or japanned in imitation of the finer woods', and as fitted with marble or marbled tops. The place of the commode was taken by a low shelved cupboard, called a chiffonier, which, as its name indicates, was of French introduction, and appears in French inventories about the middle of the eighteenth century. As described by Havard,[1] the chiffonier contained many drawers in which papers, jewels and '*chiffons*' could be stored. The name appears in Thomas Chippendale's bills for furniture supplied to Sir Edward Knatchbull for Merstham Hatch; but does not appear in print until 1806.[2] In 1808, George Smith illustrates them, in the form of low, open and shelved cupboards.[3]

In 1805, Samuel Beckwith supplied Windsor Castle with two satinwood 'chiffoniers ornamented with black lines, inlaid, with two drawers each, brass rims round tops and furniture, with locks casters and frames varnished'.[4]

They served to hold 'such books as are in constant use, or not of sufficient consequence for the library, and on the same account they become extremely serviceable in libraries for the reception of books taken for present reading'.[5]

[1] *Dictionnaire de l'ameublement*, Vol. I, p. 806.

[2] Chippendale and Haig supplied Sir Edward Knatchbull with 'a neat shiffeneer writing table japaned green and gold, with a drawer and cut bottles'.

[3] C. K. Sharpe, *Letters* (1806), 'a small, helpless family of chiffoniers, writing tables and footstools'. Chiffoniers are illustrated in George Smith's *Household Furniture* (1808).

[4] 1805. Bill of Samuel Beckwith for furniture for the drawing-room, Windsor Castle, Lord Chamberlain's Office, P.R.O.

[5] *Household Furniture* (1808), p. 21.

Mirrors

Large mirrors, hung on the walls to produce 'an endless vista', were considered a necessary part of English luxury.[1] Immense looking-glasses with gilt frames (according to Papworth's edition of the *Decorative Part of Civil Architecture*) superseded the carved and painted superstructure of the fireplace and the chimney-piece was reduced from its late magnificence 'to the duty of supporting clocks, girandoles, vases and bijoutry'. In a house in Sussex described in the *New Vitruvius Britannicus* (1802) living-rooms of very moderate dimensions were so disposed that when the large folding doors were open they made one apartment and the glasses over the chimney-pieces of the two extreme rooms gave the appearance of an 'endless suite'.[2]

The rectangular pier and chimney-glasses were often of great size during the last years of the eighteenth and early nineteenth centuries. In the saloon at the Prince of Wales's Pavilion at Brighton a large looking-glass, thirteen feet high and eight feet wide, was fixed over the chimney-piece,[3] and George Smith recommends that chimney- and pier-glasses should not have any ornament or head-pieces but be carried quite to the cornice of the room'.[4]

A number of small mirrors of architectural character were made flanked by pilasters, and surmounted by a frieze and cornice. In the upper portion there was often a painting, or mirror glass decorated with back painting.

During the eighteenth century, and especially during the later years, it was customary to have a chimney-glass above the chimney-shelf extending nearly its length. Chimney-glasses of the Regency period were flanked by pilasters and surmounted by a hollow moulding in which rows of balls were set. The upper panel was sometimes decorated in bas-relief, or by back painting, or a picture (Figs. 187, 190).

Convex mirrors, which 'strengthen the colour and take off the coarseness of objects by contracting them', had become at the date of Sheraton's *Cabinet Dic-*

---

[1] Pückler-Muskau, *Tour in Germany, Holland and England* (1826), Vol. III, p. 102.

[2] *New Vitruvius Britannicus*, Vol. I, p. 14 (1802).

[3] E. W. Brayley, *Illustrations of His Majesty's Palace at Brighton* (1838), p. 10.

[4] *Household Furniture* (1808), p. 22.

· 37 ·

tionary 'universally the fashion', and 'the perspective of the rooms in which they are suspended presents itself on the surface and produces an agreeable effect'.[1] They were made in various dimensions from about a foot in diameter to three feet, the plate enclosed in a gilt frame fitted with candle branches on either side and surmounted by an eagle displayed, a winged horse, or a finial of acanthus foliage. There was usually an ebonised fillet next the glass, a cavetto and outer band usually reeded and crossed at intervals by ribands. To the cavetto small balls were often applied at regular intervals. In the mirror from Merchant Taylors' Hall, the finial is formed by the crest of the Company, 'a lamb silver in beams gold,' resting upon entwined cornucopiae. The slightly concave border of the frame is enriched with trellis-work and in place of the usual sconce arms are female terms holding torches (Fig. 191).

Illustrations pp. 156-160.

[1] *Cabinet Dictionary* (1803), p. 271.

Lighting Fittings

After the economical illumination of the eighteenth century, the lighting of the Regency period was recognised as an advance in comfort. The new demand for adequate lighting was reinforced by the knowledge that the glass and metal which formed the chandeliers and many of the candelabra were the products of English industries which deserved to be encouraged.

Pedestals for lamps and candelabra were characteristic of the robust and Roman rendering of the classic. Candelabra of gilt wood in the music-room of Buckingham Palace were made in 1811 by Tatham, Bailey and Saunders.

The chief lighting fitting was the chandelier suspended from the ceiling. According to a writer in the *Morning Post* (1808) 'every other light, except that produced by cut-glass chandeliers is dispensed with, the candelabra and girandole being found to produce only a local light.' During the last decade of the eighteenth century, the chandelier was 'conceived as a solid'[1] and some examples were designed after a classical vase form. In the Regency period, the principle of design was 'a set of cylinders enclosing one another, and superimposed one upon another'. Each cylinder was composed of pendant 'fingers' of glass. An example of this treatment is the design made for the Emperor of China by the firm of Perry. In another pattern a glass canopy (formed of drops) descends to a rim of brass or bronze, from which lines of drops are caught up into a bowl. The angularity of many designs of this period is noted by Alison,[2] who describes the 'form of the Prism, one of the most angular of all forms', as obtaining everywhere, 'the Festoons even are angular; and instead of any winding or waving Line, the whole surface is broken into a thousand little Triangles'.

The account books of the firm of Perry contained evidence of a wide sale of English chandeliers abroad; Lord Elgin, in 1799, presented a chandelier to the Grand Seigneur, who was captivated with it, 'declaring it to be the most superb thing he ever saw and proposing to build a room on purpose for it.'[3]

The great lustres are overpowering accessories in the views of Carlton House in Pyne's *Royal Residences*. These lustres, built of ormolu hung with pendants and

[1] W. A. Thorpe, *English and Greek Glass*, Vol. I, p. 317.   [2] *Essays on Taste* (1790), p. 366.
[3] *Letters of Mary Nisbet, Countess of Elgin* (1926), p. 54.

festoons of faceted glass, are described in detail in the Carlton House accounts. Their cost was surprisingly high; in 1808 a 'magnificent fifty-six light lustre was made for the Great Drawing-room for a thousand guineas, designed to represent a fountain falling into a large reservoir'. A lustre of glass and ormolu at Carlton House is described as looking like a shower of diamonds. These lustres were supplied by Parker[1] (glass manufacturers to the Prince of Wales), whose first estimate for lustres for Carlton House is dated 1789, and who continued to provide a succession of lighting fittings displaying the Chinese, Greek and Gothic styles until Carlton House was dismantled in 1826. The immense size and cost of the lustres at Carlton House and at the Brighton Pavilion is the subject of comments in letters and journals.

Rooms were also lighted by girandoles or wall-lights, and by candelabra set upon the chimney-piece or upon pedestals. Figures carrying lights were, as in France, in fashion, and Sheraton, in his *Cabinet Dictionary*, mentions the fact that figure lights have been a recent introduction.[2]

The concealment of lights in semi-transparent alabaster vases was borrowed from France, where Madame Recamier's bedroom was 'lighted with aromatic lamps and alabaster vases' when Samuel Rogers saw it in 1802. This device is described by Warner in the same year as existing in the dining-room at Newby, in Yorkshire, where the room was lighted by several large 'transparent alabaster vases standing upon pedestals intended to receive candles'. The light of candles concealed within an alabaster vase must have been, as it is described, 'dim and religious'.[3]

Glass candlesticks and candelabra with one or more lights continued to be made with bases of varied materials. The heavy drum of marble, ormolu, earthenware, or coloured glass, gave stability to the candelabrum. In a candlestick the drum is formed of Wedgwood ware, the ovoid stem of deeply-cut glass (Fig. 210). A number of candlesticks fitted with large glass shades, painted and ground, were made in the early nineteenth century (Figs. 209, 211, 212), but, owing to the fragility of glass, few have survived.

---

[1] Parker, of Fleet Street, a firm which carried on a large business during the second half of the eighteenth century, and whose successors continued in the same line of business until lately.

[2] *Correspondence of Sarah, Lady Lyttleton*, p. 104. *Cabinet Dictionary* (1803), p. 261.

[3] R. Warner, *Tour through the Northern Counties* (1802), p. 137.

Lighting Fittings

Lamps

Lamps (vessels in which oil is burnt with a wick) were of either standard or hanging form. An improvement adopted in England about 1786 was the Argand lamp, named after its Swiss inventor, who perfected his invention between 1780 and 1783. The burner was made up of two concentric tubes carrying the wick between them, a system which allowed a double current of air, thus allowing more perfect combustion. Their advantage lies in a wick which burns around a tube fixed within a glass funnel higher than the flame with an air current beneath to prevent flickering and smoke. The container for the oil was in the case of colza, a heavy oil, placed at a higher level than the burner (or burners) so that the oil descended by gravitation.

Hanging lamps of metal were designed after antique Roman models, with spreading, boat-shaped arms connected with a vase or container for heavy oil placed at a higher level (Figs. 198, 202). The burner was protected by an upright glass shade or globe. In several cases the ornament applied to the bronze frame was gilt brass (Fig. 202). It was noted in the account books of the firm of Perry between 1812 and 1820 that burners and chains were often of French make.

Lamps were also placed on stands at a convenient height, and stands or pedestals are figured in George Smith's *Household Furniture* where it is recommended that these should be placed in the angles of drawing-rooms, or 'by the sides of large sofas, in continuation throughout the length of the room'.

In 1802 the younger Thomas Chippendale supplied Sir Richard Colt Hoare at Stourhead with 'a rich candelabrum for four lights . . . with a variety of carved ornamental work with goats' heads and lion's feet, the pillars reeded and finished in burnished gold'. Examples of similar monumental pieces exist at Castle Coole, and in the hall of Syon House (Fig. 214).

Gas as a new and revolutionary illuminant was introduced and was admired as a novelty at Lambton Hall in 1821 by Sidney Smith, who wrote that 'the splendour and glory of Lambton make all other houses mean. It is pitiful', he adds, 'to submit to a farthing candle-existence when Science puts such intense gratification within your reach. Dear Lady, spend all your fortune on a gas apparatus'.

Illustrations pp. 161-170.

Clock & Pianoforte Cases

The long-case clock is described by Sheraton in his *Cabinet Dictionary* (1803) as almost obsolete in London, and no examples are illustrated by him in this work.

The leading English clockmakers were influenced by the competition of the French makers; and a German visitor to London[1] in 1786 describes the works of Vulliamy, the Court clockmaker, as 'of exquisite beauty and perfection'. Benjamin Vulliamy was frequently in attendance upon George III at Kew, and his son, Benjamin Lewis Vulliamy (1780–1854), a man of informed taste, and a clockmaker who introduced several improvements in horology, assisted in the alterations made by the Prince of Wales at Carlton House. In a clock made by Benjamin Lewis Vulliamy for the Brighton Pavilion, about 1820, the movement is fitted into a Chinese vase of the Kang Hsi period, and surrounded by sprays of sunflowers in ormolu and flanked by kylins of the C'hien Lung period.

The designers of cases of bracket clocks assimilated the *motifs* of the day, and showed the same tendency to simplification. In the early nineteenth century the top of clocks was often lancet-shaped. Veneers of mahogany, ebony and rosewood were chiefly employed for the case, sometimes enriched by brass lines.

Act of Parliament Clocks

Large-faced wall clocks having a short case were hung in public rooms from the late seventeenth century, and to these the name of Act of Parliament clocks are sometimes given, though it is a misnomer to apply that term to a wall-clock carrying a date anterior to the year 1797 when (under William Pitt's administration) an annual tax of five shillings was imposed on all clocks, which reduced the demand by one-half. Tavern-keepers, foreseeing a scarcity of clocks and watches among their public, put up cheaply-made clocks with a large dial and drop case in prominent positions on the walls of their public rooms. The short-lived and unpopular Act was repealed in April, 1798. The Act of Parliament clocks, improvised to meet an emergency,

[1] Sophie von La Roche (*Sophie in London*, p. 100) writes: 'it is no prejudice on my part if I state that no Paris invention comes up to those which I saw here, and truly, ideas of practical value cannot be more nobly represented'. The firm of Vulliamy obtained the appointment of clockmakers to the Crown in 1742, and held it for 112 years.

have large wooden dials, usually painted black, and unglazed, and a short trunk.

Pianoforte Cases

The first pianos made in England soon after 1760 were the work of a German, Johannes Zumpe, who entered Burkat Shudi's service, and his square pianos soon became the vogue; and everyone who considered himself a person of fashion had a pianoforte as a matter of course.[1] In the late years of the century three patents were granted for upright pianofortes: Landreth's (1787), Stodart's (1795), and William Southwell's (1798). Stodart's patent was for an upright pianoforte 'in the form of a bookcase', and Haydn, who visited his shop in Lad Lane, was delighted with its new possibilities. Stodart's upright piano is a grand piano encased in a rectangular upright cupboard and placed on a stand. The case of an upright piano by Stodart from the Metropolitan Museum, New York, is of mahogany, with the name board in satinwood painted with floral swags. The upper portion is fitted with glass rods backed with white velvet painted with floral pendants and musical instruments. The four-legged stand is inlaid with stringing lines. This pattern began to go out of fashion about the end of the first quarter of the nineteenth century. The patent of William Southwell of Dublin (1798) shows a design for a square pianoforte placed on its side on a stand. An example of Southwell's upright square pianofortes (illustrated in the *Dictionary of English Furniture*, Vol. III, p. 6) has a mahogany case, banded with satinwood and rosewood, and centring in a trophy of musical instruments. The year 1800 saw the invention by two pianoforte-makers simultaneously[2] of an instrument resting 'directly upon the floor, and dispensing with a stand'. Thomas Jefferson, who visited Philadelphia in that year, writes that 'a very ingenious, modest and poor young man has invented one of the prettiest improvements in the pianoforte that I have ever seen, and it has tempted me to engage one for the Montebello. The strings are perpendicular, and he contrives within that height to give his strings the same length as in a grand pianoforte'.[3]

There is only one recorded example of Hawkins's portable grand pianoforte, which is in the possession of Messrs. Broadwood. The case is mahogany, and the pilasters at the angles are headed with Egyptian heads and finish in brass feet.

[1] Harding, R. E. M., *The History of the Pianoforte*, p. 54.
[2] Matthias Müller, of Vienna, and Isaac Hawkins, of Philadelphia.
[3] Quoted in E. Singleton, *Furniture of Our Forefathers*, p. 521.

Bedroom Furniture

The familiar types, 'four post' and 'field bed', of the late eighteenth century, were also in use in the early nineteenth century. An example of a domed state bed of this period is that at Ragley, where the dome is surmounted by antifixae and finishes in a plume of ostrich feathers. The 'field bed', named from its tent-like appearance, was lighter than the four-post bed with its cornice and tester, and the curved rods uniting the tops of the posts formed a dome above the curtains. A new pattern, the couch, or canopy or French bed, was copied from French designs, having either a low straight head and backboard, or outward curving scroll ends. In designs, this simplified structure is surmounted by a curtain supported either by a single pole fixed to the wall, or by a small tester.[1]

Chests of Drawers

The double chest of drawers was less popular during the Regency period, and George Smith describes a double chest of drawers as being made lower than usual, to 'avoid the disagreeable alternative of getting on to chairs to place anything in the upper drawers'.[2] Chests of drawers were either straight-fronted or bow-fronted. Distinctive features of the last years of the eighteenth and the early nineteenth century are the deep frieze above the top drawer, and the presence of reeded quarter columns at the front angles. About 1810–1815 spirally twisted colonettes (Fig. 218) were introduced at the front angles.

Wardrobes

When the tall double chest of drawers went out of fashion, it was superseded by a hanging press or wardrobe,[3] which in large examples consisted of a clothes press and wings.

Cheval Glasses and Dressing Glasses

The 'Psyche', or long glass raised and lowered between its uprights or swinging loosely in a standing frame, was introduced in the late years of the eighteenth

[1] G. Smith, *Cabinetmakers' Guide*, p. 182.   [2] *Household Furniture*, p. 24.

[3] A large bedroom in *Northanger Abbey* (1803) was furnished with 'a handsome family bed, . . . a bright Bath stove, mahogany wardrobe' (Chapter XXIV).

century,[1] and Sheraton illustrates an example in his *Drawing-book* which is fitted with small toilet boxes attached to the standards. The framework usually consisted of turned bars; the uprights are framed into trestle feet and connected by a stretcher (Figs. 219, 220). A cheval glass appears in Gillow's Cost books (1799) under the name of a 'screen glass frame' (Fig. 230).

In dressing glasses at the close of the eighteenth century an oblong plate took the place of the earlier shaping, and turning became the usual treatment. Those without a box stand are like cheval glasses, suspended on a frame consisting of turned uprights finishing in trestle feet tied by a stretcher. In dressing mirrors resting upon a box stand this was simplified in treatment, and the drawers fitted with bone or ivory knob handles. The stand is sometimes supported on bone or ivory knob-feet. The frame surrounding the plate is frequently of convex section in the early nineteenth century.

Dressing Tables

The dressing table with a box lid or a lifting top enclosing dressing fittings continued to be made in the last years of the eighteenth century; but with the early nineteenth century larger dressing tables, having a movable dressing glass placed on the top, became usual.

Illustrations pp. 171-180.

---

[1] The term *psyche* is said to be from Raphael's full-length painting of the fabled Psyche.—*Dictionnaire de l'Académie* (1835).

Records of Furniture Makers

ADAIR, William, carver and gilder, 26 Wardour Street, Soho, appears as one of the Royal tradesmen between 1799–1805. Adair supplied three pairs of large sofas and 'three small sofas to go between the windows' of the Great Saloon at the Queen's House in 1799 (H. C. Smith, *Buckingham Palace*, p. 92).

BAILEY, see Tatham.

BECKWITH, Samuel, of St. Martin's Lane, partner of William France, a firm which continued to be employed by the crown until the early years of the nineteenth century. The firm is included in the list of Master Cabinet-makers at the end of Sheraton's *Drawing Book*.

BLADES, John, of No. 5 Ludgate Hill, glass manufacturer, for whom, in 1816 and many subsequent years, John Papworth made designs (*Memoirs of J. B. Papworth*, 1879, pp. 37–8).

BOGAERT, Frederick (d. before 1826), a carver, born in the Low Countries, employed by Thomas Hope for furniture at Deepdene and his London house. Frederick Boeges, cabinet-maker, claimed £6 9s. for work done for the Prince Regent in 1795. In Holden's *London Directory* (1809–11) the firm is described as 'Bogaerts & Co., carvers and gilders, 23 Air Street, Piccadilly'. In George Smith's *Cabinet-Makers' and Upholsterers' Guide* (1826), Bogaert is spoken of as a carver who was also 'equally happy in his designs for furniture and other branches of interior decoration'.

BOILEAU, John James, of Sloane Square, a French painter and decorator employed in the decoration of Carlton House (1783–89). He is mentioned as one of the French craftsmen and decorators brought to England by Sheringham of Great Marlborough Street (Wyatt Papworth, *John B. Papworth* (1879), p. 11). He is described by George Smith, in his *Cabinet-maker's Guide* (1826), as having a 'light, an airy and classic style of design for household articles of comfort', and as unsurpassed in his designs for ornamental plates or articles for casting in ormolu (p. 194).

BUHL, John, of St. Martin's Lane, brazier, claimed in 1795 for braziery goods ordered and delivered at Carlton House.

BUHL FACTORY, 19 Queen Street, Edgeware Road, was owned by a Frenchman, Louis Constantin Le Gaigneur, who was active in the production of furniture in the years 1815–1816. In 1815 he supplied a 'buhl library table' for Carlton House (Carlton House Ledger).

BULLOCK (d. before 1820), a furniture-maker whose work is described in Richard Brown's *Rudiments of Drawing Cabinet and Upholstery Furniture* (1820) (p. 44), as sometimes too 'massy and ponderous'. There was great novelty without absurdity, as well as happy relief in his ornaments; nevertheless many of his articles were considerably overcharged with buhl (*Ibid.*). Miss Edgworth mentions at Aston Hall in 1820 'fine tables of Bullock's making, one of wood from Brazil, Zebrawood and no more to be had for love or money' (*Life and Letters*, Vol. I, pp. 275–6).

CAMPBELL, Robert, upholsterer and cabinet-maker, Marylebone Street, Golden Square, supplied furniture to the Prince of Wales and the Duke of York. He supplied furniture for Carlton House to the amount of £10,000 (H. C. Smith, *Buckingham Palace*, p. 104). Sheraton in his *Drawing Book* writes that 'two designs of library steps were taken from steps made by Mr. Campbell, upholsterer to the Prince of Wales, and first made for the King'.

CHIPPENDALE, Thomas, the younger (1749–1822) (the eldest child of Thomas Chippendale, the well-known furniture-maker), carried on business at St. Martin's Lane after his father's death in 1779, trading as Chippendale & Haig, until partnership was dissolved in 1796 and Haig withdrew from the firm. Chippendale visited Paris early in the nineteenth century, and a small sketch-book (formerly in the Bernal collection) is inscribed: 'sketches by Tho. Chippendale at various times'. These include ornament, chandeliers, Empire furniture sketched in Paris and in the palace at Versailles. From bills at Stourhead dating between 1795 and 1820 a number of pieces have been identified as the firm's workmanship for Sir Richard Colt Hoare, and extracts have been printed in the *Dictionary of Furniture* ('Chippendale, Thomas, junior'). The influence of French design is seen in the Stourhead furniture, *e.g.* the writing chair (*Dictionary of Furniture*, Vol. I, p. 260) is very similar to a chair by Jean Antoine Bruns, illustrated in Salverte, *Les Ebénistes du XVIIIe siècle*, plate viii. In 1819 Chippendale supplied furniture for Lord Townshend at Raynham. A letter quoted in C. Simon, from Lord Townshend, informs Chippendale that £1,200 has been placed to his account 'in payment of work done'.

Chippendale died in 1822, and in the *Cabinet Makers' and Upholsterers' Guide* (1826) George Smith speaks of Chippendale (lately deceased), known only amongst a few, 'as possessing a very great degree of taste with great ability as a draughtsman and designer'.

DECAIX (or De Caiz) Alexis, a French metal worker, mentioned in Hope's *Household Furniture* (p. 10) as having executed (with Bogaert) 'the more complicated and enriched portions' of his furniture. De Caiz's name, 'manufacturer of bronzes, 43 Old Bond Street and 15, Rupert Street,' appears in Holden's *London Directory* (1809–1811).

DAGUERRE, Dominique, a furniture dealer *à la Couronne d'Or*, in the Rue St. Honoré, Paris, where he sold, besides furniture, porcelain, glass, jewellery and *toutes sortes de curiosités*. He is mentioned in D'Oberkirch's *Memoirs* (May 25, 1784) as having at his shop a fine sideboard, which was to be sent to the Duke of Northumberland. Daguerre retired from business in the spring of 1793 (Salverte, *Les Ebénistes du XVIII siécle*, p. 75) and came to London. He claimed £15,500 for himself and for his partner Legreieux of Sloane Street, for furniture sold to the Prince of Wales and delivered to Carlton House in the proceedings of the Commissioners for the Prince of Wales' debts (1795). Furniture supplied by him has been identified at Buckingham Palace (see H. C. Smith, *Buckingham Palace*, Plates 169 and 170).

DOMINIQUE (Dominic), Jean, of Marshall Street, gilder and brass founder, who executed work in ormolu for Carlton House between 1783 and 1786 (H. Clifford Smith, *Buckingham Palace*, p. 103). He claimed a small sum of £13 17s. 6d. for work at Carlton House in the proceedings of the Commissioners for the Prince Regent's debts (1795).

ELLIOTT, Charles, upholsterer and cabinet-maker. John Elliott, upholsterer, New Bond Street, appears among the subscribers to Sheraton's *Cabinet Dictionary* (1803). Much furniture was supplied by the firm for William Tufnell at Langleys between 1797 and 1798. Charles Elliott (1752–1832) appears in *Directories* 1784–1808. The firm appears at 97 New Bond Street, and subsequently 1808–1826 at No. 104, under various styles (*Country Life*, January 23rd, 1942).

FOLHGAM, John. This maker's name is given at first in Wood Street, and later in Fleet Street. A card of his and also a bill head, are in the Heal collection (information supplied by Sir Ambrose Heal). 'Folqham, cabinet-maker' appears in the account of Samuel Whitbread, for Southill.

GAUBERT, Guillaume, of Panton Street, 'maker of ornamental furniture' claimed £1133 19s. 8d. for ornaments at Carlton House' in 1795. When Horace Walpole visited Carlton House in 1785 he attributed the decorations at Carlton House to 'Gobert'.

GILLOW, the firm of (of Lancaster and London), founded by Robert Gillow, a joiner who moved to Lancaster from Kirkham-in-the-Fylde, and was in 1728 made a Freeman of Lancaster. In 1757 Robert's son Richard was taken into partnership, and about 1765 land was leased and premises built on the site of the present showrooms of Messrs. Waring & Gillow. In 1790 the firm was Robert Gillow & Co., upholders, in 1807 G. and R. Gillow & Co., merchants, cabinet-makers, etc. Not many years later the Gillows ceased to be connected with the business, though it was still carried on under their name. Richard Gillow (d. 1811), who in 1800 took out a patent for an improved dining-table, did much to extend and consolidate the business. His son, Richard Thomas Gillow, retired from the business in 1830.[1] Clark, in his *Historical and Descriptive Account of Lancaster* (1807), writes that the town had 'long been famous for the great quantities of mahogany furniture which have been made in it for home use and exportation. Mr. Gillow's extensive warerooms, stored with every article of useful and ornamental mahogany furniture, are well worth the attention of the stranger, as they are said to be the best stocked of any in this line out of the metropolis'. A German visitor to London speaks (in 1807) of George and Richard Gillow among the 'first-grade manufacturers in London:[2] their work is good, and solid though not of the first class in inventiveness and style'.

[1] *Gillows, a Record of a Furnishing Firm* (1901).   [2] P. A. Nemwick, *Neueste Reise durch England* (1807).

Among furniture bearing the stamp of the firm is a gilt couch in the Victoria and Albert Museum (Fig. 77).

HERVÉ, Francis, 'French chairmaker', of John Street, Tottenham Court Road (*Universal British Directory*, 1790–1793), appears among the craftsmen employed at Carlton House between 1783 and 1786, the amount of his bill being £1,275 17s. 7d. (H. Clifford Smith, *Buckingham Palace*, p. 103). The total estimate of his work amounted in 1789 to £3,000 (*Ibid.*). In a bill from him at Althorp he charges Lady Spencer:

1789. To a fauteuil à la Raine in wenscott	£2	3	6
1791. To six Cabriole Backstools made to match a canopy Bedstead @			
£2 7 6	14	5	0
To two tête-à-tête to match @ £3 13	7	6	0

A combined table and set of library steps in the Victoria and Albert Museum, dating from about 1790, is by him.

INCE AND MAYHEW, a firm which ranked high among the cabinet-makers of the second half of the eighteenth century. The name of William Ince, cabinet-maker, appears among the subscribers to the *Director* (1754). The name of the firm is well known because of the existence of their *Universal System of Household Furniture*, published in 1759. A set of mahogany chairs by the firm were made in 1792 for the Westminster Fire Office, and are still in the possession of this Company. Their address on the title page is Broad Street, Soho. In the *London Directories* Ince & Mayhew are first mentioned in Broad Street in 1778, being described as 'cabinet-makers, upholsterers and dealers in Plate Glass'. In 1781 the firm moved to Marshall Street, Carnaby Market, where they remained until the early nineteenth century. In the *Universal British Directory* (1803) the number is given as 47, and in Holden's *Directory* (1809–1811) as 48, Marshall Street.

LE-GAIGNEUR, Louis, see Buhl factory.

LICHFIELD (or Litchfield), with Graham as partner appear in *London Directories* at 15 St. Martin's Lane 1783–1784. In *Directories* 1790–1793, the firm appears as Litchfield and Graham, 72 St. Martin's Lane. Payment to Lichfield, Morell and Co. is entered in the Southill accounts in 1798; and to Graham, upholsterer in 1808.

McLEAN. The name of John McLean, cabinet-maker appears in the Westminster *Poll Book* (October, 1774). He issued a trade card on which his name is rendered 'Jas. Macklane, cabinet, chair-maker and upholsterer in Little Newport Street near Leicester Square'. A later trade card which was issued from Upper Marylebone Street, indicates that he specialised in Elegant Parisian furniture (Banks Collection, British Museum). The name of McLean & Son, Upper Terrace, Tottenham Court Road and 34 Marylebone Street, Piccadilly appears on the list of cabinet-makers and the *Cabinet Dictionary* (1803), where the design for a work table is said to be 'taken from one executed by Mr. McLean in Marylebone Street, who finishes these small articles in the neatest manner'. The *London Directories* (1809–1814) give the names of John McLean & Son, upholders, at 58 Upper Marylebone Street, and after 1814 the firm's style is William McLean (see letter from Sir Ambrose Heal, *Country Life*, September 3rd, 1943, p. 430). A cabinet bearing McLean's label is in the Victoria and Albert Museum (Murray Collection) shows a considerable amount of brass mounts (Fig. 153).

MOREL, Nicholas, cabinet-maker, of Tenterden Street, is first mentioned in the accounts of the Commissioners for the Prince of Wales' debts (1795), in which he submitted a claim for £192. In 1802 he was established at 13, Great Marlborough Street. In Holden's *London Directory* (1809–1811) the firm's style is Morel & Hughes, upholsterers and cabinet-makers, 13, Great Marlborough Street. In the accounts preserved at Southill, £2,167 4s. 3d. was paid in 1798 to Lichfield, Morell & Co. and in 1800, £1,580 7s. 5d. was paid to Morell, Marsh, etc. In 1804 £306 was paid to Morell, etc., upholsterers and £550 11s. 2d. in 1805. Small sums were paid in 1806, 1807 to the firm. In Ackermann's *Repository* (1825) mention is made of 'magnificent furniture' recently made for the Duke of Northumberland by Morel & Hughes. Morel later joined the firm of Seddon, and in the *London Directory* of 1832 the name appears as Seddon, Morel & Seddon. (*See* SEDDON.)

MORGAN AND SAUNDERS, a firm which was established in 1801 and by 1809 had executed 'very extensive orders for a vast variety of furniture'. An illustration of their showrooms in Catherine Street, the Strand, appears in Ackermann's *Repository* (August, 1809). The firm named their manufactory Trafalgar House after Nelson's victory. The firm is described as 'sofa, bed, and chair manufacturers, upholsterers and cabinet-makers, 15, 16 and 17, Catherine Street', in the *Post Office Directory*, 1815.

MARSH, William, the name of Marsh, upholder and cabinet-maker, Mount Street, appears in the *London Directory* (1778). Some furniture at Southill, Bedfordshire, is stated in a letter of the Rev. Samuel Johnes (written in 1800) to be by Marsh, whose 'cabinets are superb', and who had 'made some frames for the glasses with a large bead that has a very good effect on the gilding' (Jourdain, *Decoration and Furniture of the Late Georgian Period*, p.217). A portion of a mirror with a large bead in Mrs. Whitbread's boudoir is illustrated in *Country Life*, December 7, 1929, p. 844. In the proceedings of the Commissions for the Prince of Wales' debts (1795), the firm is described as 'William Marsh & Co., upholders'. In 1802 the firm's style is Elward, Marsh & Tatham. (*See* TATHAM.)

At Southill, Marsh worked from Holland's designs, or from designs made in his office.

OAKLEY. The *Journal des Luxus und der Moden* (in 1801) speaks of 'everyone of taste and discrimination making their purchases at Oakley's, the most tasteful of London's cabinet-makers', and in 1807 a German visitor writes that Oakley & Co. 'have not such far-reaching business [as the firm of Gillow], but they are the best-known for articles in the latest taste.

Their warehouse is one of the sights of London' (P. A. Nemwick, *Neueste Reise durch England*, 1807).

The name of George Oakley, upholsterers and cabinet-makers, 22, St. Paul's Churchyard, first appears in London *Directories* in 1790 and continues there until 1795. In 1796 the firm appears as Oakley & Kettle, at the same address. In 1799 the firm appears as George Oakley, and in 1800 as Oakley, Shackleton & Evans, 8 Old Bond Street and St. Paul's Churchyard.

The name of George Oakley (cabinet-maker) appears among the subscribers to Sheraton's *Cabinet Dictionary* (1803). The address of George Oakley, cabinet-maker and upholsterer, is given in Holden's *London Directory* (1809–1811) as 22, St. Paul's Churchyard and 8, Old Bond Street.

From a manuscript inventory of the furniture supplied by George Oakley in 1810 for Papworth Hall, Cambridgeshire, a number of pieces (inherited by Mrs. Stileman) can be identified (*Architectural Review*, 'English Empire Furniture made by George Oakley'). The following extracts from this account include the more important pieces:

'An elegant satinwood winged wardrobe fitted with drawers and clothes shelves, and enclosed with panelled doors, formed of choice woods and elaborately inlaid with ebony.'

£75

'The mahogany winged library case in the Grecian style, the door fitted with brass trellis wire and quilled silk curtains, with best locks and keys.'   £47 5

'A capital mahogany sideboard supported on a stand, reeded legs and carved and bronzed paw feet with antique bronze heads.'   £26

'A calamanderwood circular loo table upon pedestal and claws, the top inlaid with a border of stars in brass and ebony."   £31 10 6

PARKER, glass manufacturers, 8 Fleet Street, a firm founded by William Parker in 1756. In 1804 the firm's style was Perry & Parker, and in that year they corresponded with Sir Roger Newdigate about chandeliers supplied by them in 1788. The name changed to Perry & Co. in 1817, when the business was transferred to 78 New Bond Street. The firm possessed drawings for chandeliers dating from about 1790 until the accession of George IV, together with the names of their clients and the prices paid. Among the clients were Sir Roger Newdigate (1804), the Emperor of China (1811).

PARKER, Thomas, of 18 Air Street, Piccadilly, a cabinet-maker who specialised in 'Boulle' furniture.

ROBINS, John, Warwick Street, Golden Square, supplied furniture for the Bank of England (Bolton, *Sir John Soane's Museum*, p. 133) in the early years of the nineteenth century.

RUSSELL, John, joiner and chair-maker, who was established in New Bond Street between

1776 and 1810, was chair-maker to the King (*Kent's Directory* and the *Universal British Directory*). In 1800 he supplied St. James's Palace with 6 mahogany chair-frames with carved vase and feather backs, moulded feet to match, £9 18s. He supplied to the Prince Regent in 1808:

'a double-headed couch bedstead richly carved with figures and ornamented Egyptian heads, gilt leaves, chased honeysuckles, lyres.' £209 10

Quoted in *The Burlington Magazine*, November, 1915 (vol. 28, p. 79).

SEDDON, a large and very important firm of furniture-makers, founded by George Seddon (a son of John Seddon of Blakelea and Eccles in Lancashire), who was born in 1727 and came to London about 1750,[1] and set up business in Aldersgate as a cabinet-maker. His name appears in 1754 among the subscribers to *Chippendale's Director* (1st edition). In *Kent's Directory* (1768) his address is given as 158, Aldersgate Street, but in the 1770–1784 editions of this directory the number is given as 151. After 1784, the number is given as 150. In 1785 he seems to have taken his son, also named George, into partnership, and the firm's style appears as George Seddon & Son. This was changed in 1789 to George Seddon & Sons.

A German visitor to London in 1786 thus describes the firm: 'He employs four hundred apprentices on any work connected with the making of household furniture—joiners, carvers, gilders, mirror-workers, upholsterers, (founders) . . . who mould the bronze into graceful patterns—and locksmiths. All these are housed in a building with six wings. In the basement mirrors are cast and cut. Some other department contains nothing but chairs, sofas and stools of every description, some quite simple, others exquisitely carved and made of all varieties of wood, and one large room is full up with all the finished articles in this line, while others are occupied by writing-tables, cupboards, chests of drawers, charmingly fashioned desks, chests, both large and small, work and toilet tables in all manner of woods and patterns, from the simplest and cheapest to the most elegant and expensive. . . . Seddon, foster-father to four hundred employees, seemed to me a respectable man, a man of genius too. [He] has appreciated the value of all his own people's labour and toil and is for ever creating new forms'.[2]

In a description of Mr. William Bingham's house in Philadelphia (1794), the drawing-room chairs are described as 'from Seddon's in London, of the newest taste, the back in the form of a lyre'.

From 1793 to 1800 the firm's style is George Seddon, Sons, & Shackleton.[3] Shackleton died or left the firm in 1801, and in 1802 the style reverts to Seddon & Sons on the death of the first George Seddon, in 1801; in 1804 the firm changed its name to Thomas and George Seddon. Thomas, the senior partner, dying in 1804, his name drops out of the directories, and the business is carried on under the name of George Seddon. In 1816 and 1817 George Seddon

---

[1] Seddon, *Memoirs and Letters of the late Thomas Seddon* (1858), p. 2.

[2] *Sophie in London* (1786), pp. 173–5, published 1933.

[3] The new partner, Thomas Shackleton, had married Mary Seddon.

and Thomas his (nephew) are given as tenants of 150 Moorgate Street; and on the death of the senior partner, George, in 1818, the name of Thomas Seddon only appears. From 1820 to 1836 Thomas and George (his younger brother) were at 149–150 Aldersgate Street, and in 1826 they opened a West End branch at 16 Lower Grosvenor Street, where they were joined by Nicholas Morel (*q.v.*). In 1832 the Directory gives the style of the firm as Seddon, Morel & Seddon. In the following year (1833) Thomas and George Seddon opened premises in Gray's Inn Road, and in 1837 they transferred their business to these premises, vacating the Aldersgate Street premises.

Between 1826 and 1830 Messrs. Morel & Seddon supplied upwards of £200,000 worth of furniture for Windsor Castle (H. C. Smith, *Buckingham Palace*, p. 159 note, and *Country Life*, October 21, 1933). The account was investigated after George IV's death, and the firm received only £179,300, signing the last receipt, November 12, 1831. A table by the firm of Seddon is illustrated.

SHERATON, Thomas (1751–1806). Most of what is known of Thomas Sheraton is chiefly based on scant information from his works. He was born in humble circumstances at Stockton-on-Tees (1751). He is first heard of not as a mechanic but as a Baptist, and on the title-page of his book, *A Scriptural Illustration of the Doctrine of Regeneration*, he describes himself as a 'mechanic, one who never had the advantages of a collegiate or academic education'. In 1791–1794 he issued the *Cabinet-makers' and Upholsterers' Drawing-book* (which passed through two subsequent editions), and containing some 111 copperplates. A *Cabinet Dictionary* published in 1803 is illustrated with 88 copperplates, and contains a list of 252 cabinet-makers in and about London; of his last-projected work, the *Cabinet-makers', Upholsterers' and General Artists' Encyclopaedia*, only one volume appeared (1805). His trade card (*Dictionary of English Furniture*, Vol. 3, p. 118), which gives his address as 106, Wardour Street, Soho, states that he 'teaches Perspective, architecture and ornaments, makes designs for Cabinet-makers'. He died at Broad Street, Soho, in 1806, and the *Gentleman's Magazine*, in an obituary notice, states that he had been for 'many years a journey-man cabinet-maker; but since the year 1793 . . . has supported himself by his exertions as an author'.

SMITH, George, cabinet-maker and designer, who published in 1808 (being then in business in Princes Street, Cavendish Square) a *Collection of Designs for Household Furniture and Interior Decorations*, with Preliminary Remarks, in which he speaks of the recent 'propitious change' in furniture design which has 'arisen from a more close investigation and imitation of the beautiful remains of ancient sculpture and painting'. He tells us that his designs were 'studied from the best antique examples of the Egyptian, Greek and Roman styles' but some specimens in the Chinese taste are added. A chair with lion-head terminals (Fig. 34) and a dressing table (Fig. 217, 233) closely resemble designs in his book. In 1812 he issued a *Collection Ornamental Designs* 'after the manner of the antique' (in which the 'purest antique ornament' is 'accommodated to modern embellishment'). The collection consists chiefly of ornamental *motifs* for the metal worker, carver and statuary, but there are two designs for pedestals, a tripod and a chair 'after the antique'. His *Cabinet-makers' and Upholsterers' Guide* (1826) is issued from Brewer Street, Golden Square. In this work he writes that he has had an experience of forty years, both in the theory and practice of cabinet-making, and had been patronised by George IV and received testimonies from Thomas Hope, and describes himself as 'upholsterer and furniture draughtsman to his Majesty and principal of the drawing Academy, Brewer Street, Golden Square'. In the preface he writes that his *Designs for Household Furniture* (1808) had become wholly obsolete by the change of taste during the last twenty years.

TAITT, Richard, upholsterer, 92, Jermyn Street, St. James's, appears in London *Directories* in 1788 and continues until 1800; became one of the Royal tradesmen in 1793 (Lord Chamberlain's accounts, P.R.O.).

TAITT, John, upholsterer and cabinet-maker, 75, Swallow Street, Piccadilly, first appears in London *Directories* at this address in 1779, and continues there until 1785, when he moves to 254 Oxford Street, where he continues until 1800. (He is listed among the Royal tradesmen in H. Clifford Smith, *Buckingham Palace*, p. 277.)

TATHAM, Thomas, of 13, Mount Street, was the eldest son of Ralph Tatham (d. 1779) and brother of the architect, Charles Heathcote Tatham. He joined the firm of William Marsh of Mount Street, and the firm from 1795 was the principal cabinet-makers to George, Prince of Wales. Tatham became head of the firm of Marsh & Tatham in 1809, and shortly afterwards the firm's style was Tatham and Bailey, upholsterers to his Royal Highness the Prince of Wales, of 14, Mount Street (Holden's *Directory*, 1809–1811). The sum of £1,695 10s. 3d. was paid to 'upholsterer, Tatham, etc., in 1801 in the Southill accounts, and a further sum £3,737 15s. 5d. is entered in 1802 as paid to Tatham, Morell, etc. In 1809 £1,120 9s. 10d. is paid to Tatham and in the following year £1,162 13s. 5d. In 1811, £1,154 9s. 3d. is entered in the firm's account, and in 1812 £1,070 11s. 9d. In 1811 the firm was Tatham, Bailey & Saunders (H. C. Smith, *Buckingham Palace*). In 1817 the firm was Bailey & Saunders. Examples of the furniture of this firm are shown in Chapter I. Thomas Tatham died in 1818 at Brighton, leaving an estate to the value of £60,000 (*Gentleman's Magazine*, Jan. 1, 1818).

VULLIAMY, (the firm of), a well-known firm founded by Justin Vulliamy, partner of Benjamin Gray, who obtained the appointment of clock-maker to the Crown in 1742. In 1786, a German visitor, who paid a visit to Vulliamy's, 'witnessed works of exquisite beauty and perfection there. It is no prejudice on my part to state that no Paris invention comes up to those which I saw here; and truly, ideas for practical use cannot be more nobly represented' (*Sophie in London*, 1786, p. 100). Benjamin Lewis Vulliamy (1780–1854), third in succession of this famous family, introduced several peculiarities and improvements into the clocks made by the firm. He was made free of the Clockmakers' Company in 1809, admitted to the Livery in 1810, and five times filled the office of Master. 'He was a man of refined taste in art, and possessed no small knowledge of architecture, painting and engraving.' Benjamin Lewis Vulliamy from 1806 onwards was employed by the Prince of Wales not only on the repairing and making of clocks, but on the making and repair of metal work, mounts and objects of all kinds (H. Clifford Smith, *Buckingham Palace*, p. 113). A pair of candelabra at Harewood House, having ormolu candle-branches springing from a black marble column mounted with lion masks, and resting on a base of ormolu and ebony, is signed Vulliamy, London, 1811.

Illustrations pp. 181-184.

Illustrations

The Greek Revival

FIG. 1. OCCASIONAL TABLE the top of plum-pudding mahogany containing a panel and mosaic of hard stones, the legs mounted with ormolu. *c.* 1800. From S. Whitbread, Esq., Southill.

Height, 2 feet $3\frac{1}{2}$ inches.
Width, 2 feet $8\frac{5}{8}$ inches.

FIG. 2. WRITING TABLE with rosewood top. The panel ground of the supports painted green and mounted with ormolu, the scrolled base carved and gilt.

Height, 2 feet 6 inches.
Length, 3 feet 3 inches.
c. 1800.

58

FIG. 3. CHINA CUPBOARD of rosewood, mounted with ormolu columns and applied ornament (by Marsh & Tatham). *c.* 1800. From S. Whitbread, Esq., Southill.

FIG. 4. ROSEWOOD COMMODE par[...]
with ebony and mounted with ormolu. Fro[...]
Whitbread, Esq., Southill.

Height, 2 feet 10¼ inches.
Width, 3 feet 9½ inches.
Depth, 8½ inches.

FIG. 5. ROSEWOOD COMMODE mounted
with ormolu, and fitted with a gallery (of similar
design to fig. 4). From Headfort, Ireland.

Height (to top of gallery), 4 feet ½ inch.
Width, 4 feet 2 inches.

FIG. 6. GILT SOFA, with ormolu mounts (part of a set). From S. Whitbread, Esq., Southill.

FIG. 7. GILT ARMCHAIR (part of a set) and rosewood footstool mounted with ormolu. *c.* 1805. From S. Whitbread, Esq., Southill. Height (of chair), 2 feet 9¾ inches. Width, 1 foot 11⅝ inches. Stool. Height (of stool), 7 inches. Width, 1 foot 5 inches.

FIG. 8. WHITE MARBLE CHIMNEY from the drawing-room, Southill, and chimney glass with carved and gilt frame and panel enriched with the Greek acanthus foliage relieved against a green ground (originally of green velvet). *c.* 1800. From S. Whitbread, Esq., Southill.

FIG. 9.
ROSEWOOD WRITING-
TABLE with tambour front
and ormolu mounts. *c.* 1800.
From S. Whitbread, Esq.,
Southill.

Height, 3 feet 4 inches.
Width, 3 feet 5½ inches.

FIG. 10.
ROSEWOOD COMMODE
(one of a pair) mounted with
ormolu (the design by Holland
in the R.T.B.K.) *c.* 1800. From
S. Whitbread, Esq., Southill.

Height, 3 feet 4 inches.
Length, 5 feet 6½ inches.

63

FIG. 11. ROSEWOOD BOOKCASE mounted with ormolu, made in 1806 (by Marsh & Tatham).
From the Royal Collection, Buckingham Palace. Height, 5 feet 7 inches. Length, 5 feet 2 inches.

FIG. 12. DESIGN FOR A COUCH from Hope's 'Household Furniture and Interior Decoration' (1807).

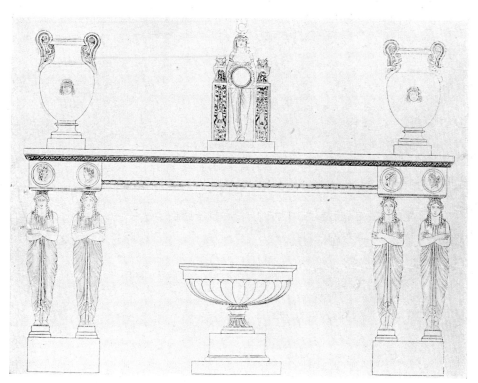

FIG. 13. DESIGN FOR A SIDETABLE from Hope's 'Household Furniture and Interior Decoration' (1807).

FIG. 14. MAHOGANY BOOKCASE designed by Thomas Hope for Deepdene in the Egyptian taste. The Egyptian heads to the pilasters are carved and painted and the applied ornaments to the frieze and cupboards are in bronze of a dull green tint. *c.* 1805. From James Watson-Gandy-Brandreth, Esq., Buckland Newton.

Fig. 15. Top of table (Fig. 16).

Fig. 16. MAHOGANY TABLE, inlaid with ebony and silver, designed by Thomas Hope for Deepdene. *c.* 1807. From the Victoria and Albert Museum. Height, 2 feet 4⅜ inches.

FIG. 17. A PAIR OF MAHOGANY TRIPOD STANDS supported by lion monopodia (formerly at Chumber). *c.* 1807. From the Victoria and Albert Museum. Height 2 feet 9 inches. Diameter of top, 1 foot 8 inches.

FIG. 18. ROSEWOOD TABLE with hinged section to the top and Egyptian supports, having heads and feet of brass. *c.* 1807. From the Earl of Sandwich, Hinchingbrooke.

FIG. 19. KNEE HOLE LIBRARY TABLE, painted with figures and ornament in the classic taste, and having the cupboards flanked by Egyptian terms. From Julians. Width, 6 feet. Depth, 4 feet ¼ inch.

FIG. 20. A COUCH WITH CROCODILE LEGS. The frame carved and painted bluish-green with gilt detail. *c.* 1810. From Mrs. Clement Williams.

FIG. 21. ROSEWOOD TABLE of Carlton House type. The Egyptian heads of brass. *c.* 1807. From the Earl of Sandwich, Hinchingbrooke.

FIG. 22. SECRETAIRE veneered with light mahogany and inlaid with dark wood. *c.* 1810. From Ralph Dutton, Esq., Hinton Ampner House. Height, 4 feet 9 inches. Width, 3 feet 2 inches.

FIG. 23. DETAIL OF A PIER TABLE (one of a pair) of ebony mounted with ormolu. Formerly in the Chinese drawing-room, Carlton House. *c.* 1790. From the Royal Collection, Buckingham Palace. By gracious permission of His Majesty the King.

FIG. 24. PIER TABLE (one of a pair) of ebony with ormolu mounts, made about 1790 from a design by Holland and shown in an engraving of the Prince of Wales's Chinese drawing-room at Carlton House. The figures of Chinamen painted and gilt. From the Royal Collection, Buckingham Palace. By gracious permission of His Majesty the King. Height, 3 feet 1½ inches. Length, 5 feet 4 inches.

FIG. 25. SHELVED CABINET with framework in imitation of bamboo and cupboard doors japanned in the Chinese taste in black and gold. The claw feet gilt. Made for the Pavilion, Brighton. From Basil Ionides, Esq., Buxted Park. Height, 3 feet 1½ inches. Length, 7 feet 10 inches.

FIG. 26. The cabinet, showing the centre cupboard open.

FIG. 27. COMMODE inlaid with ebonised lines and mounted with panels of lacquer and pseudo-Chinese inscriptions. *c.* 1800. From the Earl of Caledon, Caledon, Ireland.

Height, 3 feet 3¾ inches.
Length, 4 feet 3¼ inches.

FIG. 28.
JAPANNED COMMODE decorated in gold on a black ground, with carved and gilt balusters and feet. *c.* 1810. From Henry Channon, Esq.

Height, 2 feet 2½ inches.
Width, 3 feet 6¼ inches.

FIG. 29. CARVED AND GILT THRONE CHAIR (one of a pair) for Carlton House, from the Throne Room, Buckingham Palace, the back carved with acanthus scrolls and foliations. *c.* 1813. Height, 3 feet 6 inches. Width, 3 feet.

Fig. 30.
PAINTED ARMCHAIR with caned seat and oval back panel
filled in with a diagonal lattice. *c.* 1801.

Fig. 31. PAINTED ARMCHAIR with caned seat and oval
panel painted with a figure subject. *c.* 1795.

FIG. 32.
PAINTED ARMCHAIR with caned seat and back. From Basil Ionides, Esq., Buxted Park. Height, 2 feet 11½ inches. Width, 1 foot 10¼ inches.

FIG. 33.
ARMCHAIR PAINTED GREEN the top rail painted with flowers. From Basil Ionides, Esq., Buxted Park. Height, 2 feet 10½ inches. Width, 1 foot 10¼ inches.

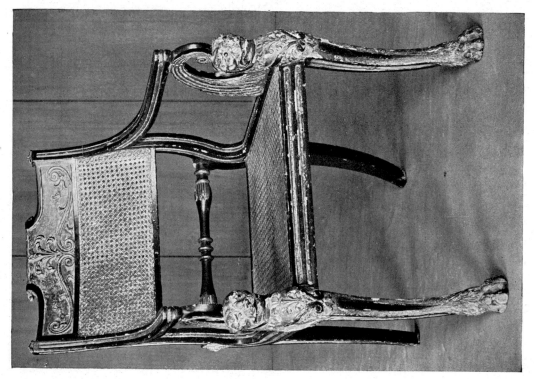

FIG. 35. PAINTED AND GILT ARMCHAIR with caned seat and back panel, the front legs formed as winged lion monopodia. (By George Smith). c. 1810. From H. Goodhart Rendel, Esq. Height, 2 feet 9¼ inches. Width, 1 foot 10 inches.

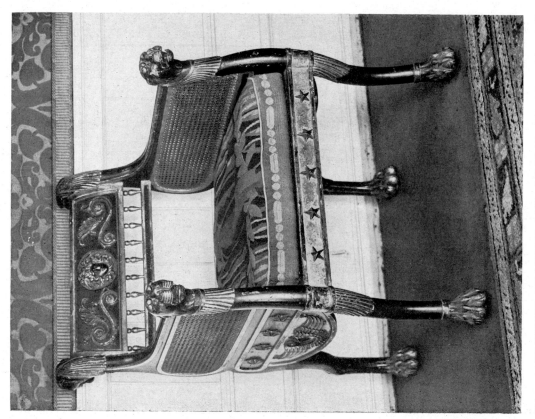

FIG. 34. PAINTED, BRONZED AND GILT ARMCHAIR with caned seat and arms, designed by George Smith, and illustrated in his 'Household Furniture' (1808), the plate being dated 1804.

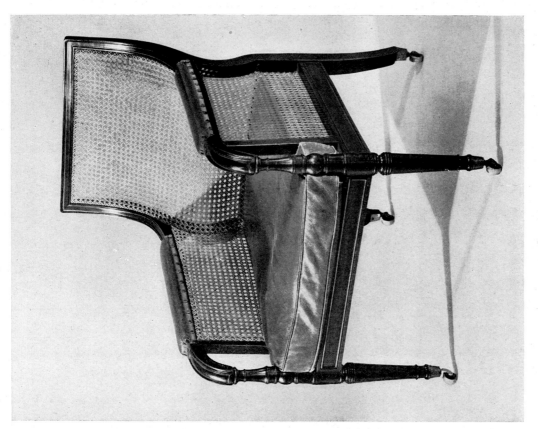

FIG. 37. MAHOGANY BERGÈRE with caned back, seat and arms. *c.* 1800. From Lord Yarborough, Brocklesby Park. Height, 3 feet 1½ inches. Width, 2 feet 1 inch.

FIG. 36. MAHOGANY CANED BERGÈRE made for Sir Richard Colt Hoare by Thomas Chippendale, junior, in 1816. From Sir Henry Hoare, Bart., Stourhead.

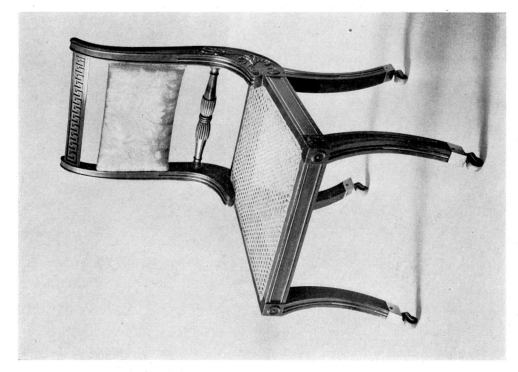

FIG. 39. MAHOGANY SINGLE CHAIR with caned seat. c. 1805. From Lord Yarborough, Brocklesby Park. Height 2 feet 10½ inches. Width, 1 foot 8 inches.

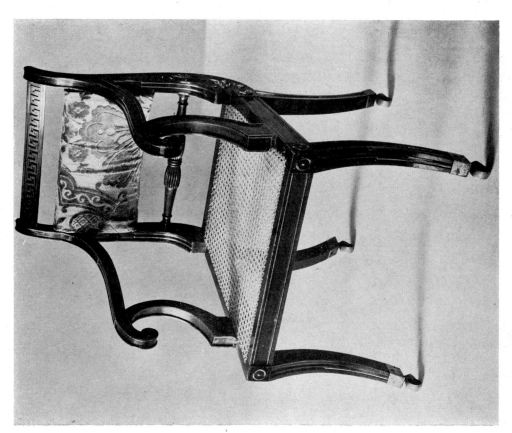

FIG. 38. MAHOGANY ARMCHAIR with caned seat. c. 1805. From Lord Yarborough, Brocklesby Park. Height, 2 feet 10½ inches. Width, 1 foot 10 inches.

FIG. 41. PAINTED ARMCHAIR with caned seat, the panel in centre of the back painted with a classical group. The junction of the front legs and arm supports formed by a turned column. *c.* 1805.

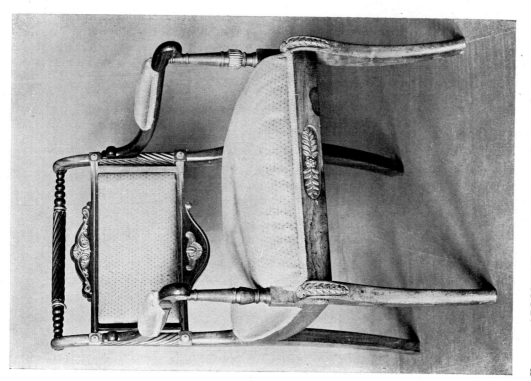

FIG. 40. ARMCHAIR with spiral turned sections to uprights and top rail and carved panels on leg and seat rail. *c.* 1805. From Denston Hall.

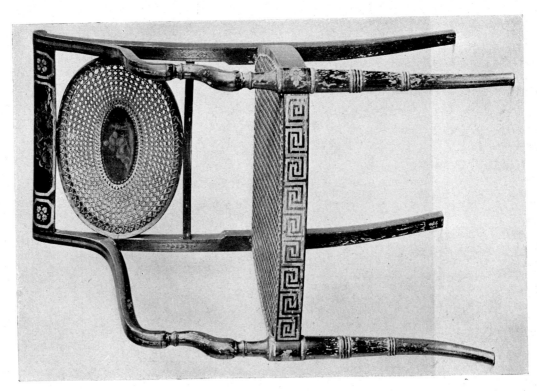

Fig. 42. SATINWOOD ARMCHAIR inlaid with ebony lines, having caned seat and diagonal crossing to the back. Made by Thomas Chippendale, junior, in 1802 for Sir Richard Colt Hoare. From Sir Henry Hoare, Bart, Stourhead.

FIG. 41. PAINTED ARMCHAIR with caned seat, the panel in centre of the back painted with a classical group. The junction of the front legs and arm supports formed by a turned column. *c.* 1805.

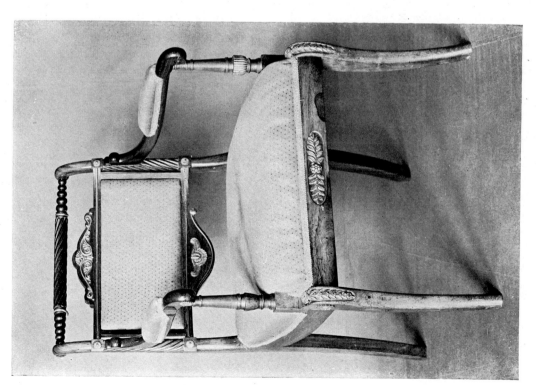

FIG. 40. ARMCHAIR with spiral turned sections to uprights and top rail and carved panels on leg and seat rail. *c.* 1805. From Denston Hall.

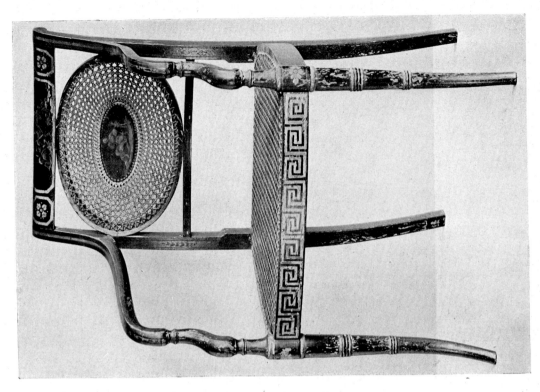

FIG. 43. ARMCHAIR OF BEECH, painted, with caned seat. In centre of the back is a medallion decorated with a figure painting surrounded by concentric caning. *c.* 1800. From the Victoria and Albert Museum. Height, 2 feet 8¾ inches. Width, 1 foot 9¼ inches.

FIG. 42. SATINWOOD ARMCHAIR inlaid with ebony lines, having caned seat and diagonal crossing to the back. Made by Thomas Chippendale, junior, in 1802 for Sir Richard Colt Hoare. From Sir Henry Hoare, Bart., Stourhead.

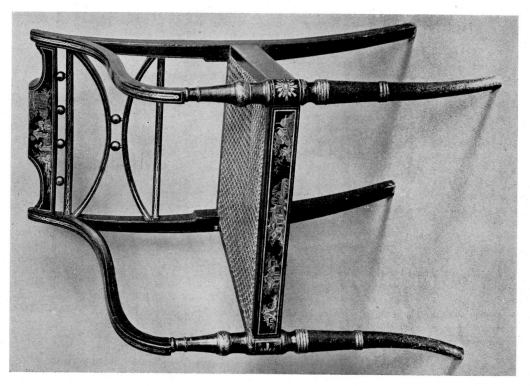

FIG. 45. ARMCHAIR OF BEECH, japanned black and decorated with gilt ornament in the Chinese taste. From Halnaby Hall. Height, 2 feet 8¼ inches. Width, 1 foot 9¾ inches.

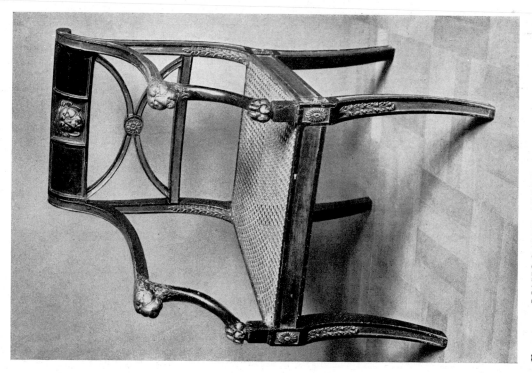

FIG. 44. MAHOGANY ARMCHAIR. *c.* 1805. From H. Goodhart Rendel, Esq. Height, 2 feet 11½ inches. Width 2 feet ¼ inch.

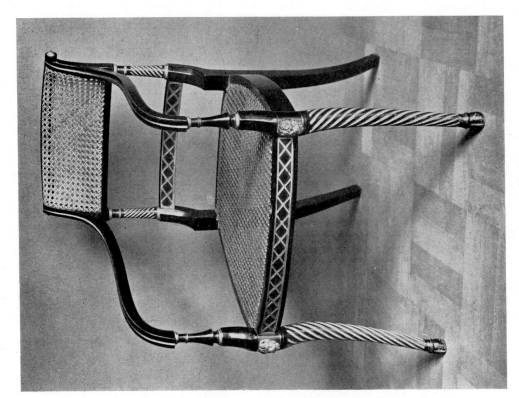

FIG. 47. ARMCHAIR with gilt enrichments and caned seat and back panel. Early 19th century. From H. Goodhart Rendel, Esq. Height, 2 feet 9 inches. Width, 1 foot 9½ inches.

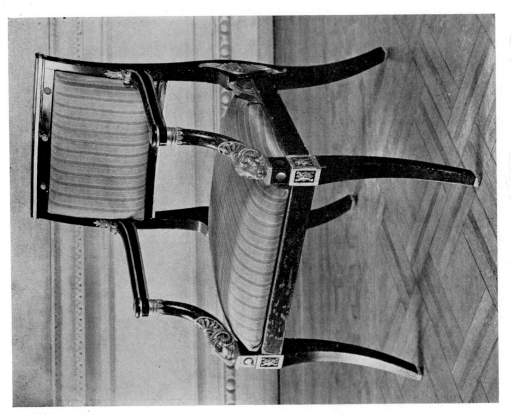

FIG. 46. PAINTED ARMCHAIR, with carved and gilt details. From the Earl of Bradford, Weston Park. Height, 2 feet 11¼ inches. Width, 1 foot 10 inches.

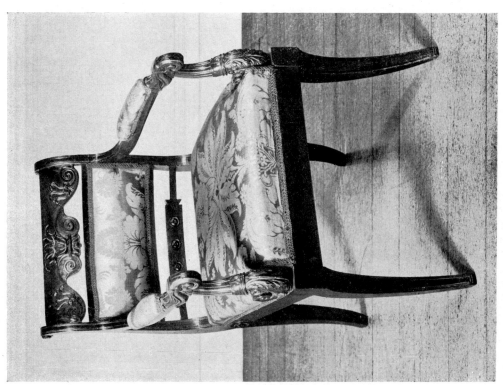

FIG. 49. MAHOGANY ARMCHAIR with carved top rail and arm supports. *c.* 1805. From Lord Yarborough, Brocklesby Park. Height, 2 feet 9½ inches. Width, 1 foot 9¾ inches.

FIG. 48. MAHOGANY UPHOLSTERED ARMCHAIR with carved top rail and arm supports. *c.* 1805. From Lord Yarborough, Brocklesby Park. Height, 3 feet 1½ inches. Width, 2 feet 5 inches.

FIG. 50.
MAHOGANY SPOON-BACK CHAIR. *c.* 1800. From Earl of Caledon, Caledon, Ireland.

Height, 2 feet 11 inches.
Width, 1 foot 9½ inches.

FIG. 51.
PAINTED CHAIR with spoon back. From Browsholme Hall, Yorkshire.

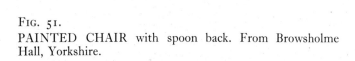

Height, 2 feet 11½ inches.
Width, 1 foot 9¾ inches.

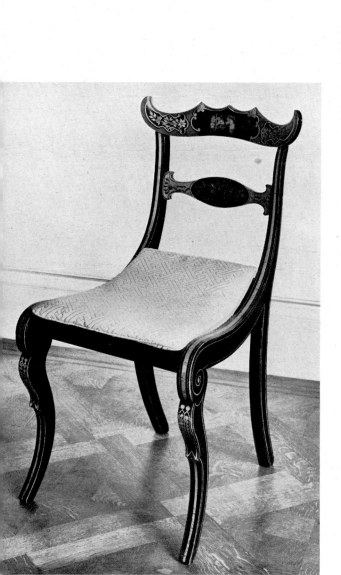

FIG. 53.
SINGLE CHAIR, japanned black with gilt details (see Fig.
74). Early 19th century. From Henry Channon, Esq.

    Height, 2 feet 9½ inches.
    Width, 1 foot 6 inches.

Fig. 54.
SINGLE CHAIR with caned seat and framework painted and bronzed. From Basil Ionides, Esq., Buxted Park.

Height, 2 feet 8¾ inches.
Width, 1 foot 6⅝ inches.

Fig. 55.
SINGLE CHAIR japanned in black and gold in the Chinese taste. *c.* 1810. From Mrs. Gordon Woodhouse.

Height, 2 feet 10¾ inches.
Width, 1 foot 6¾ inches.

FIG. 56.
MAHOGANY SINGLE CHAIR inlaid with ebonised lines
(the back panel originally mounted with crocodile in metal).
c. 1810. From the Duke of Richmond, Goodwood House.

FIG. 57.
MAHOGANY ARMCHAIR with lion front legs. *c.* 1805.
From Clough Williams-Ellis, Esq.

Height, 2 feet 10½ inches.
Width 2 feet.

H

FIG. 58.
GILT ARMCHAIR. *c.* 1805. From the Earl of Caled‹
Caledon, Ireland.

Height, 3 ft. 2 inches.
Width, 2 ft. 7 inches.

FIG. 59.
MAHOGANY ARMCHAIR with gilt lion paw terminals
arm supports. *c.* 1800. From Ralph Dutton, Esq., Hin‹
Ampner House.

Height, 3 feet 2½ inches.
Width, 2 feet 1½ inches.

FIG. 60.
ARMCHAIR painted black with gilt details. Early 1‹
century. From Henry Channon, Esq.

Height, 2 feet 10½ inches.
Width, 1 foot 11¾ inches.

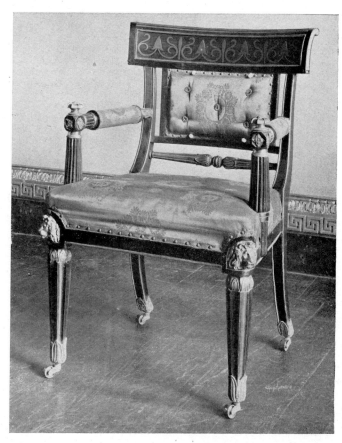

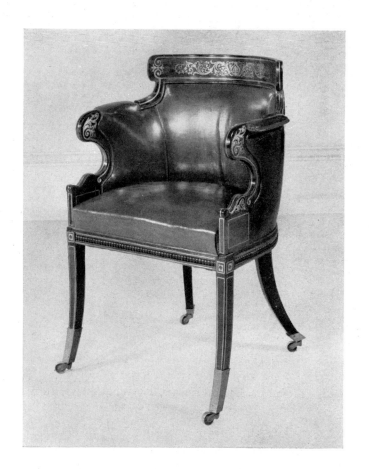

61.

HOGANY SINGLE CHAIR with inlay black wood.
05. From the Earl of Bradford, Weston Park.

ight, 2 feet 8 inches.
dth, 1 foot 7 inches.

62.

HOGANY ARMCHAIR with gilt enrichments. *c.* 1815.
the Town Hall, Liverpool.

ight, 3 feet.
dth, 2 feet.

63.

HOGANY ARMCHAIR upholstered in leather and
with brass. *c.* 1820. From the Bank of England.

FIG. 64. PAINTED SOFA. *c.* 1800. Height, 2 feet 10 inches. Length, 7 feet.

FIG. 65. COUCH PAINTED IN IMITATION OF ROSEWOOD with gilt enrichments. *c.* 1815.
From Mrs. Edward Haynes, The Mill Cottage, Burford. Height, 2 feet 9 inches. Length, 6 feet 1½ inches.

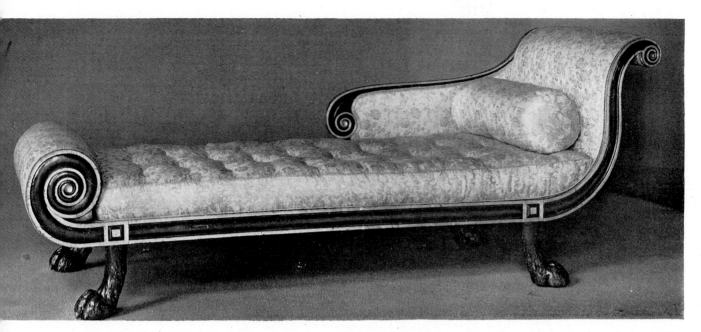

. 66. PAINTED SOFA OF COUCH FORM, with gilt mouldings. *c.* 1810. From the Earl of Jersey, Osterley Park. Height, :et 9½ inches. Length, 7 feet.

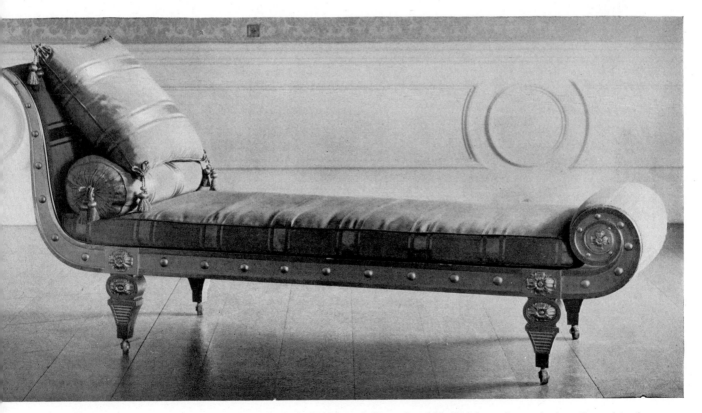

FIG. 67. GILT SOFA (one of a pair). *c.* 1800. From S. Whitbread, Esq., Southill. Height, 2 feet 11 inches. Length, 7 feet.

FIG. 68. PAINTED AND CANED SOFA. *c.* 1810. From Sir Roderick and Lady Jones.

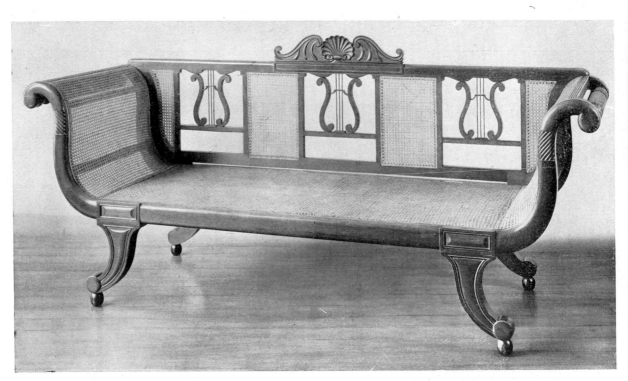

FIG. 69. MAHOGANY SOFA. *c.* 1810. From the Thomas-Stanford Museum, Brighton. Height, 2 feet 10 inches. Length, 8 feet.

;. 70. SOFA (one of a pair) japanned black with gilt decoration. *c.* 1800. From Ronald Tree, Esq., Ditchley. Height, 2 feet
nches. Length, 5 feet.

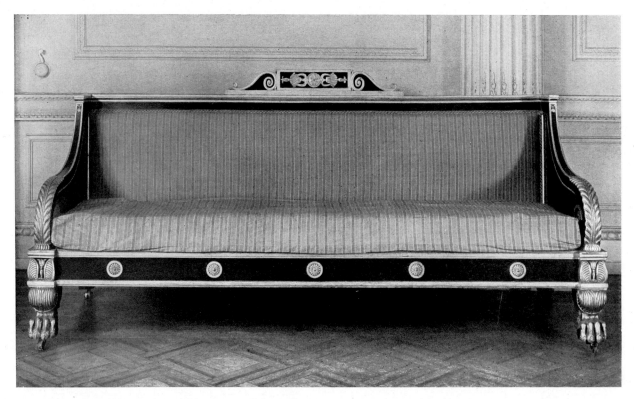

FIG. 71. SOFA with carved and gilt details. Early 19th century. From the Earl of Bradford, Weston Park. Height, 3 feet. Length, 6 feet 4½ inches.

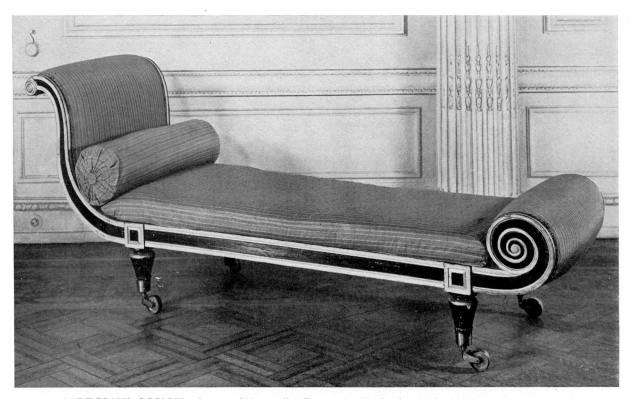

FIG. 72. 'GRECIAN' COUCH, the mouldings gilt. From the Earl of Bradford, Weston Park. Height, 2 feet 10 inches. Length, 7 feet.

FIG. 73. MAHOGANY SOFA. *c.* 1800. Height, 2 feet 10 inches. Length, 6 feet 2½ inches.

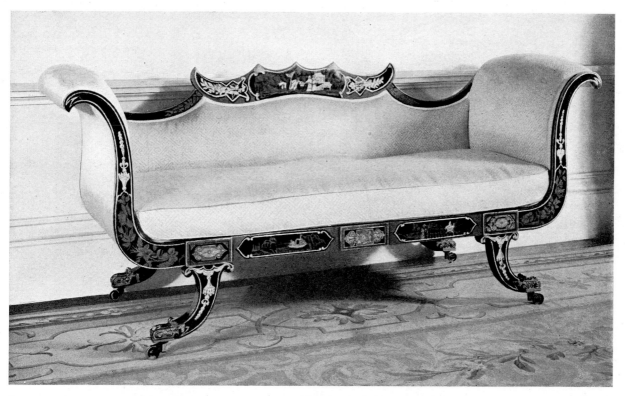

FIG. 74. SOFA OF BEECH, japanned black, and decorated with gilt detail (see Fig. 53). Early 19th century. From Henry Channon, Esq. Height, 2 feet 11 inches. Length, 6 feet 8½ inches.

FIG. 75. ROSEWOOD COUCH inlaid with ornament in brass. *c.* 1810.

FIG. 76. PAINTED SOFA with gilt enrichments. *c.* 1800. From Sir Roderick and Lady Jones.

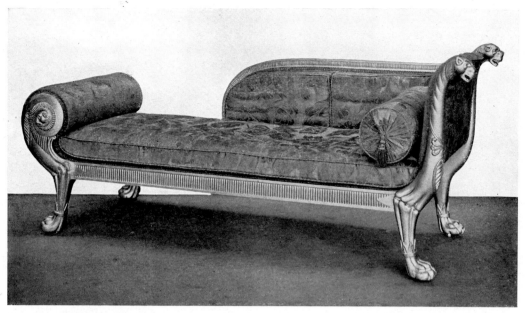

FIG. 77. COUCH of carved and gilt wood, the uprights at the head formed as lion terminals and the scrolled end carved with lion masks, with lion supports (part of a set made by Gillow in 1805). From the Victoria and Albert Museum. Height, 2 feet 8½ inches. Width, 6 feet 8 inches.

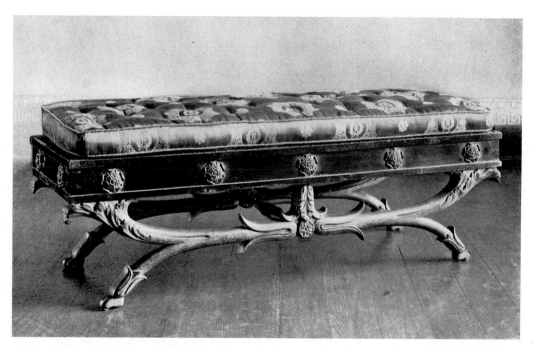

FIG. 78. LONG STOOL with gilt enrichments and underframery. Early 19th century. From the Town Hall, Liverpool. Height, 1 foot 6 inches. Length, 3 feet 10 inches.

FIG. 79. CROSS-FRAMED GILT STOOL. *c.* 1810. From the Duke of Northumberland, Syon House.

FIG. 80. PAINTED FOOTSTOOL with lion feet. *c.* 1810. From the Duke of Devonshire, Chatsworth. Height, 10 inches. Length, 1 foot 5 inches.

FIG. 81. FOOTSTOOL ENTIRELY COVERED WITH HAND-PAINTED VELVET and fitted with brass claw and ball feet. *c.* 1810. From Basil Ionides, Esq., Buxted Park. Height, 8½ inches. Width, 1 foot 6 inches.

FIG. 82. MAHOGANY FOOTSTOOL of couch form. Height, 9½ inches. Length, 1 foot 4½ inches.

G. 83. GILT SEAT with cross frame. *c.* 1805. From the Duke of
rthumberland, Syon House.

FIG. 84. MAHOGANY CROSS-FRAMED STOOL.
c. 1800. Height, 1 foot 3½ inches. Width, 1 foot 9 inches.
From Ralph Dutton, Esq., Hinton Ampner House.

FIG. 85. PAINTED CROSS-FRAMED SEAT with gilt enrichments.
c. 1807. From the Viscount Allendale, Bretton Park. Height, 2 feet
4¼ inches. Width, 2 feet, 6½ inches.

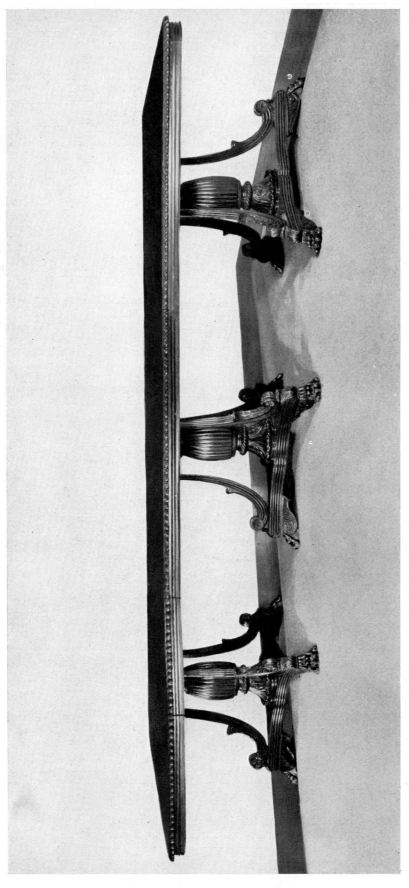

FIG. 86. MAHOGANY DINING TABLE with three tripod supports. Early 19th century. From Hotspur, Richmond.

FIG. 87. MAHOGANY DINING TABLE on two supports. *c.* 1800. From F. D. Lycett Green, Esq., Finchcocks.

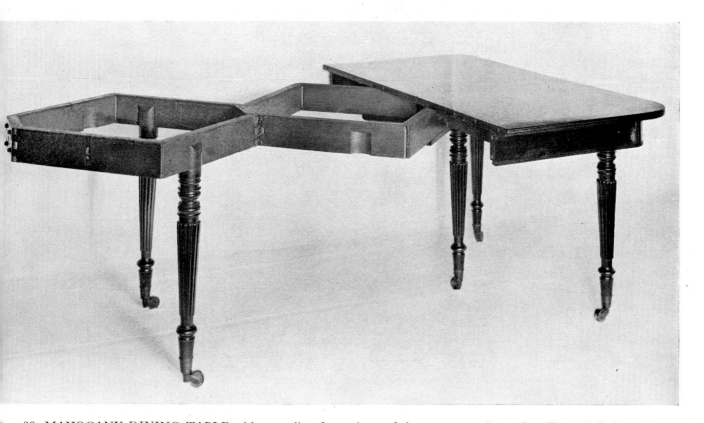

IG. 88. MAHOGANY DINING TABLE with extending frame (part of the top removed). *c.* 1810. From F. Seddon, Esq.

FIG. 89. MAHOGANY SIDETABLE with frieze inlaid with ebonised lines and ornament. (One of a pair). *c.* 1810. From the Duke of Richmond, Goodwood House.

FIG. 90. ROSEWOOD DINING-ROOM SIDETABLE (one of a pair). Part of a set of five sidetables. From S. Whitbread, Esq., Southill.

Fig. 91. SLAB OF SCAGLIOLA forming the top of console table (Fig. 92).

Fig. 92. CONSOLE TABLE supported by carved gilt lion monopodia, the top formed of a slab of scagliola (Fig. 91). *c.* 1800. From Ralph Dutton, Esq., Hinton Ampner House. Height, 2 feet 11 inches. Width, 4 feet 1½ inches.

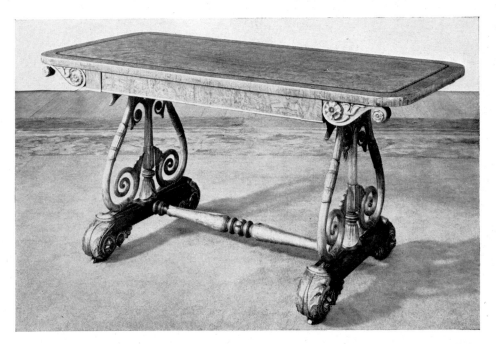

Fig. 93. TABLE with gilt supports and carved and gilt details. *c.* 1810. From Ralph Dutton, Esq., Hinton Ampner House. Height, 2 feet 4½ inches. Length, 4 feet 10½ inches.

Fig. 94. MAHOGANY TABLE, the top decorated in pen and ink on a prepared ground, and dated 1815. From the Victoria and Albert Museum. Height, 2 feet 4¼ inches. Length 5 feet 1¾ inches.

FIG. 95. SOFA-TABLE with lyre supports, the ground stained black leaving the ornament in the natural white wood. From Lord Doverdale. Height, 2 feet 4½ inches. Length, 4 feet 11½ inches.

FIG. 96. SOFA-TABLE of amboyna inlaid with brass, made in 1816 for Princess Charlotte. (One of three.) From the Royal Collection, Buckingham Palace. By gracious permission of His Majesty the King. Height 2 feet 4¼ inches. Length, (extended), 4 feet 9 inches.

Fig. 97. MAHOGANY SOFA-TABLE banded with satinwood and resting on lyre supports. Made by the younger Thomas Chippendale. *c.* 1800. From Sir Henry Hoare, Bart., Stourhead. Height, 2 feet 5 inches. Length (extended), 5 feet 6 inches.

Fig. 98. SOFA-TABLE OF ZEBRA WOOD. Made in 1810 by George Oakley. From Mrs. Stileman. Height, 2 feet 3½ inches. Length (extended), 5 feet.

Fig. 99. ROSEWOOD TABLE mounted with gilt brass busts at the angles. *c.* 1800 (see Fig. 135). From the Earl of Sandwich, Hinchingbrooke.

Fig. 100. MAHOGANY SOFA-TABLE inlaid with ebonised stringing lines. *c.* 1795. From the the Earl of Shaftesbury, St. Giles's House.

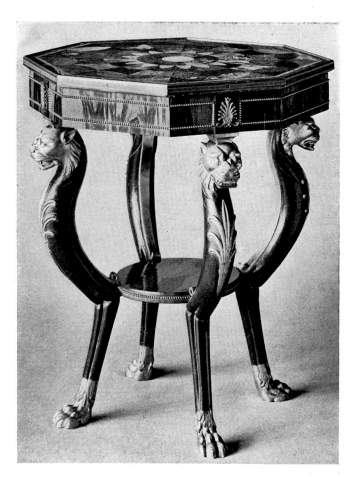

FIG. 101.
OCTAGONAL ROSEWOOD TABLE the top of inlaid marble. The lion monopodia are parcel-gilt, the frieze and platform mounted with brass. *c.* 1805. From the Marquess of Northampton, Castle Ashby.

Height, 2 feet 7 inches.
Length, 2 feet 1½ inches.

FIG. 102.
CIRCULAR TABLE veneered with zebra wood, with gilt paw feet. *c.* 1810. From Ralph Dutton, Esq., Hinton Ampner House.

Height, 2 feet 5 inches.
Diameter of top, 4 feet.

FIG. 103. MAHOGANY SIDETABLE with carved terminal supports, the frieze and terms mounted with gilt brass enrichments. *c.* 1800. From the Earl of Bradford, Weston Park. Height, 2 feet 11 inches. Length, 4 feet 3½ inches.

FIG. 104. GILT SIDETABLE with gryphen supports. From 20, St. James's Square, London.

Tables

FIG. 105.
MAHOGANY PIER TABLE
dwarf bookcase) supported by win
lion monopodia. Early 19th cent
From the Earl of Bradford, Wes
Park.

Height, 3 feet 1½ inches.
Length, 4 feet 11¾ inches.

FIG. 106.
PIER TABLE with marble top and
gilt details. *c.* 1810. From the Earl of
Caledon, Caledon, Ireland.

Height, 2 feet 10 inches.
Length, 4 feet 4½ inches.

FIG. 107.
MAHOGANY CARD TABLE
(one of a pair) inlaid on top and
frieze, the standard partly decorated
with gilding, and the feet bronzed.
Early 19th century. From Viscount
Allendale, Bretton Park.

Height, 2 feet 4½ inches.
Width, 3 feet.

FIG. 108.
TABLE with folding top and
carved and gilt dolphin supports,
part of a set given in 1813 in
memory of Lord Nelson. From
Admiralty House, Whitehall,
London.

Height, 2 feet 5½ inches.
Length, 3 feet 2 inches.

Fig. 109. TABLE JAPANNED BLACK with top forming a chess or draughtsboard. *c.* 1800. From Ston Easton.

Fig. 110. CARD-TABLE VENEERED WITH BURR ELM (one of a pair) with folding top inlaid with ebonised lines, the rosettes to the scroll supports of carved wood. *c.* 1810. From the Duke of Wellington. Height, 2 feet $5\frac{1}{4}$ inches.

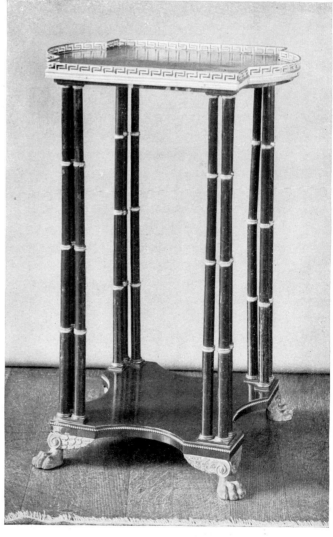

Fig. 111.
ROSEWOOD TABLE with lyre supports, inlaid with brass lines. *c.* 1795.

Fig. 112.
TABLE WITH ROSEWOOD TOP and base, and painted bamboo supports (the top mounted with a brass gallery). *c.* 1800. From the Earl of Shaftesbury, St. Giles's House.

FIG. 113.
PAINTED TRIPOD TABLE (dated 1805 on top). Mrs. R. Tree.

FIG. 114.
OCCASIONAL TABLE (one of a pair), with rosewood top, brass gallery, the centre support gilt and carved in an Egyptian taste. *c.* 1810. From S. Whitbread, Esq., Southill. Height, 2 feet 5 inches.

FIG. 115.
SATINWOOD DRUM WRITING-TABLE. From S. Whitbread, Esq., Southill.

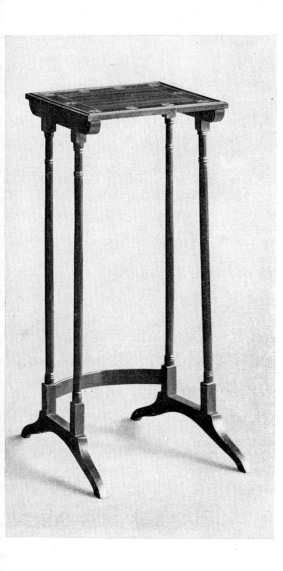

Fig. 117.
SET OF MAHOGANY QUARTETTO
TABLES the tops inlaid with brass stars. *c.* 1810.
From Mrs. Stileman.

Height (enclosed), 2 feet 5 inches.
Length, 1 foot 6 inches.

FIG. 118. ROSEWOOD WORK-BOX on stand. *c.* 1810. From the Earl of Shaftesbury, St. Giles's House.

FIG. 119. ZEBRA WOOD COMBINED WORK AND GAMES TABLE fitted with a pouch, and with slide inlaid with a chessboard. *c.* 1800. From Mrs. Stileman. Height, 2 feet 5½ inches. Length, 2 feet 6 inches.

FIG. 120   FIG. 121

FIGS. 120, 121. MAHOGANY GLOBE-SHAPED WORK-BOX decorated with the signs of the Zodiac engraved on a band of ebony; the legs of ebonised wood, panel gilt, From Buckingham Palace. *c.* 1810. Height, 3 feet.

Fig. 122.
ROSEWOOD DRUM-TOPPED TABLE on tripod stand. *c.* 1795. From the Thomas-Stanford Museum, Brighton.

Height, 2 feet 4½ inches.
Diameter of top, 1 foot 5 inches.

Fig. 123.
SATINWOOD URN-TABLE with painted decoration. Dated 1790. From the Victoria and Albert Museum.

Height, 2 feet 4½ inches.
Width of top, 1 foot 2½ inches.

FIG. 124. MAHOGANY LIBRARY TABLE (very similar to a library table in Sheraton's *Drawing Book* (179). From H. M. The King's apartments, Windsor Castle.

FIG. 125. MAHOGANY LIBRARY TABLE, the frieze inlaid in brass on an ebony ground, the doors mounted with bronze enrichments, and the pilasters with bronze capitals and feet. *c.* 1800. From Captain Musker. Height, 4 feet. Length, 7 feet.

FIG. 126. SABICU LIBRARY TABLE with carved frieze, enrichments on the panels and terminal figures. From the Victoria and Albert Museum. Height, 2 feet 7 inches. Length, 9 feet 0½ inches.

FIG. 127. MAHOGANY LIBRARY TABLE made by Thomas Chippendale, junior, for Sir Richard Colt Hoare. 'A large mahogany library table with pedestals and drawers under pedestals, mahogany panelled doors, thermed legs with philosopher's heads carved on do., four end therms with Egyptian heads.' (Thomas Chippendale's bill, 1805.) From Sir Henry Hoare, Bart. Stourhead. Height, 2 feet 6½ inches. Length, 8 feet 3 inches.

FIG. 128. SATINWOOD CARLTON HOUSE TABLE. Height, 2 feet 11¾ inches. Length, 4 feet 6¾ inches.

FIG. 129. MAHOGANY CARLTON HOUSE TABLE with tapered legs headed by a tassel capping. From M. Harris & Sons.

FIG. 130. ROSEWOOD WRITING-TABLE with bronzed lion-headed cross-supports. The top is bordered with a brass gallery and the drawers mounted with a brass beading. *c.* 1805. From S. Whitbread, Esq., Southill.

FIG. 131. ROSEWOOD WRITING-TABLE with bronzed legs. *c.* 1800. From S. Whitbread, Esq., Southill.

FIG. 132. TABLE VENEERED WITH ZEBRA WOOD. Early
19th century. From Ralph Dutton, Esq., Hinton Ampner House.

FIG. 133. ROSEWOOD TABLE fitted with a brass gallery. *c.* 1800. From S.
Whitbread, Esq., Southill. Height, 2 feet 7¾ inches. Length, 3 feet 4 inches.

FIG. 134. PAINTED WRITING-TABLE, the carved details coloured green to resemble bronze. The capitals of the legs gilt. *c.* 1800. From the Earl of Morley, Saltram. Height, 2 feet 4 inches. Length, 2 feet 9 inches.

FIG. 135. ROSEWOOD TABLE, mounted with gilt brass busts at the angles (see Fig. 99). *c.* 1800. From the Earl of Sandwich, Hinchingbrooke. Height, 2 feet 6½ inches. Length, 3 feet ¼ inch.

FIG. 136.
MAHOGANY LIBRARY TABLE, the frieze fitted for books and mounted with a brass moulding. (Formerly at Devonshire House.) *c.* 1800. From the Duke of Devonshire.

FIG. 137.
MAHOGANY TABLE having hinged sections to the top. *c.* 1800. From the Marquess of Northampton, Castle Ashby.

FIG. 138.
MAHOGANY OCTAGONAL WRITING TABLE. 1800. From F. D. Lycett Green, Esq., Finchcocks.

FIG. 139. ROSEWOOD WRITING-TABLE. *c.* 1805. From Lord Huntingfield, Heveningham Hall. Height, 2 feet 5 inches. Length, 5 feet.

FIG. 140. LIBRARY TABLE with brass ring handles, the frieze fitted for books, the feet carved gilt. *c.* 1820. Formerly at Normanton Park.

FIG. 141.

MAPLEWOOD TABLE AND BOOKCASE
with bronzed enrichments. From Robert Tritton,
Esq., Godmersham Park.

Height, 2 feet 6½ inches.
Diameter of top, 3 feet.

FIG. 142. DRUM-SHAPED TABLE veneered with light mahogany and inlaid in
dark wood. Early 19th century. From Ralph Dutton, Esq., Hinton Ampner House.
Height, 2 feet 6 inches. Diameter of top 4 feet 9 inches.

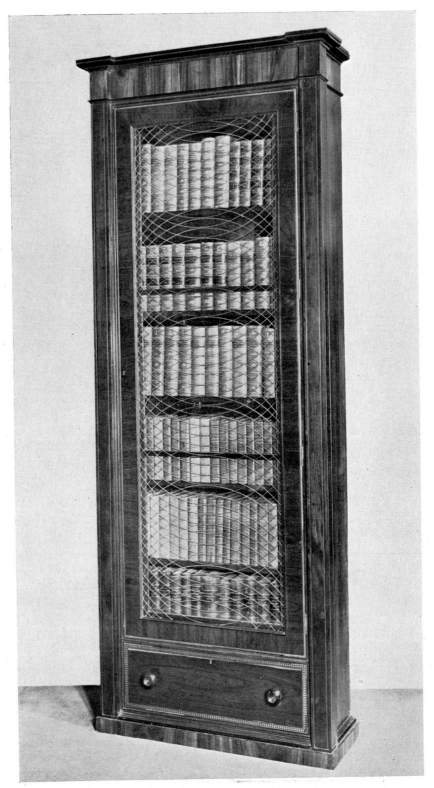

FIG. 143. MAHOGANY BOOKCASE (one of a pair) with door fitted with brass wire trellis. From Leonard Knight, Esq.

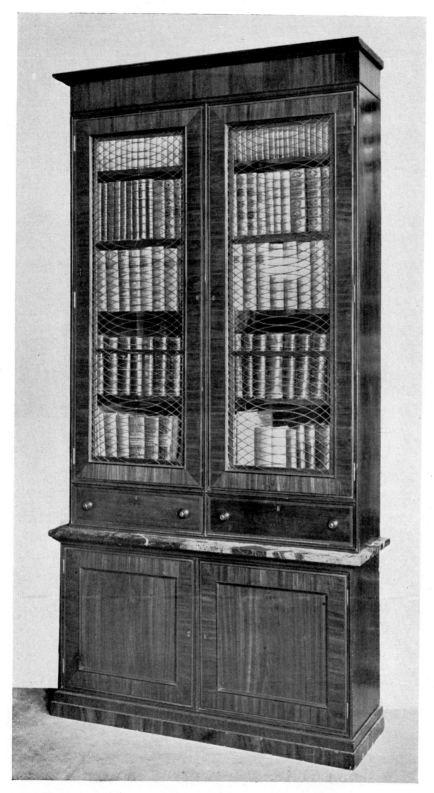

FIG. 144. MAHOGANY BOOKCASE with doors fitted with brass wire trellis. From Leonard Knight, Esq.

FIG. 145. A PAIR OF BOOK SHELVES, painted black and decorated on the base with small figures. Early 19th century. Frou Leonard Knight, Esq.

FIG. 146. MAHOGANY DWARF BOOKCASE. Height, 2 feet 11½ inches. Length, 4 feet 2⅝ inches.

FIG. 147.
SECRÈTAIRE CABINET of mahogany, veneered with zebra wood, the pilasters on the lower stage mounted with Egyptian heads and feet in ormolu. The water-colour drawings in the glazed upper stage are signed Baynes, 1808. *c.* 1808. From the Victoria and Albert Museum.

Height, 5 feet 2½ inches.
Width, 2 feet 6¾ inches.

FIG. 148.
MAPLEWOOD CABINET cross-banded with tulip wood, the sides panelled with engraved ebony. The cupboard doors are enclosed by a wire mesh.

Height, 4 feet 7¾ inches.
Width, 2 feet 5 inches.

Fig. 149. MAHOGANY BOOKCASE shelved on either side. *c.* 1800. From
Lord Leconfield, Petworth.

FIG. 150.
ROSEWOOD BOOKCASE (one of a pair) with colonettes of gilt wood, resting on a plinth decorated in imitation of porphyry. From the Duke of Wellington.

Height, 3 feet 2½ inches.
Width, 5 feet.

FIG. 151.
MAHOGANY BOOKCASE with gilt lion monopodia, surmounted by a marble slab. *c.* 1810. From Mrs. Clement Williams.

FIG. 152. LOW BOOKCASE veneered with zebra wood, divided by reeded pilasters mounted with brass lion masks. From
Earl of Yarborough, Brockelsby Park. Height, 2 feet 11¾ inches. Length, 5 feet 6½ inches.

Fig. 153. ROSEWOOD SECRETARY, surmounted by two tiers of brass shelves and mounted with gilt brass. There is a secretary drawer with a falling front, the interior fitted with pigeon holes and three drawers. By John McLean. *c.* 1810. From the Victoria and Albert Museum. Height, 4 feet 9¾ inches. Width, 3 feet ½ inch.

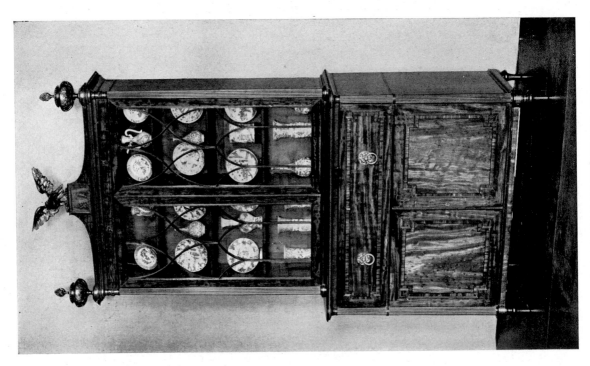

FIG. 155. MAHOGANY SECRÈTAIRE CABINET with glazed upper stage, the cornice surmounted by a carved and gilt eagle and two flammate urns. *c.* 1800.

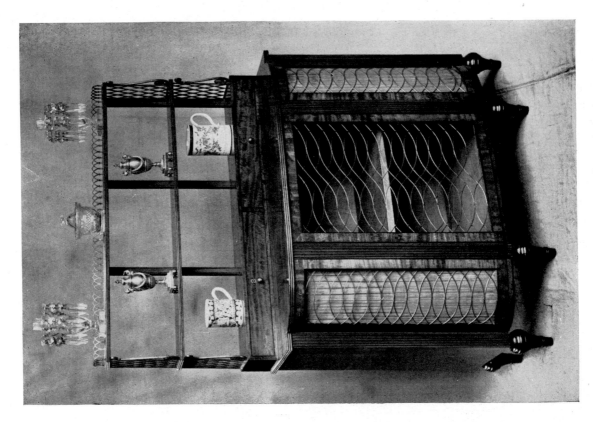

FIG. 154. MAHOGANY CUPBOARD with shelved superstructure fitted with a brass gallery. The cupboard doors fitted with wire trellis.

FIG. 157. MAPLE BOOKCASE inlaid with ebony, fitted with a marble top with a brass gallery. *c.* 1800. From the Earl of Shaftesbury, St. Giles's House.

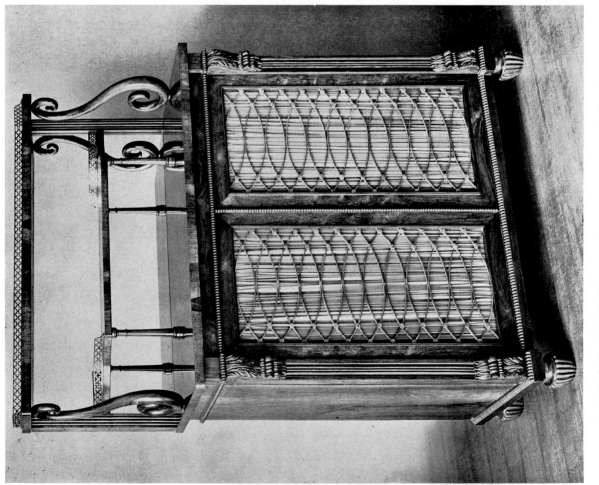

FIG. 156. ROSEWOOD CABINET (one of a pair) with wire trellis doors. *c.* 1815. From the Thomas-Stanford Museum, Brighton. Height, 3 feet (to top of cabinet). Height of superstructure, 1 foot 4½ inches. Width, 3 feet.

FIG. 158.
MAHOGANY REVOLVING BOOK SHELVES
on a table stand. *c.* 1800.

FIG. 159.
MAHOGANY REVOLVING BOOKCASE. *c.*
1800.

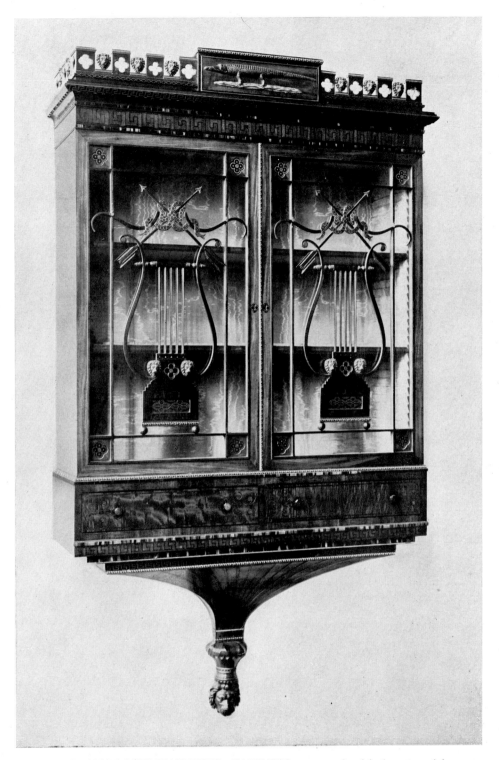

FIG. 160. MAHOGANY HANGING CABINET, mounted with brass enrichments.
[The brass mount of a crocodile on the tablet commemorates the Battle of the Nile, 1797.]
c. 1797. From the Victoria and Albert Museum. Height, 6 feet 2½ inches. Width, 3 feet
9⅜ inches.

Bookcases and Bookshelves

FIGS. 161, 162.
MAHOGANY LIBRARY CHAIR AND STEPS
combined. By Morgan & Saunders. *c.* 1811. From
Trinity College, Oxford.

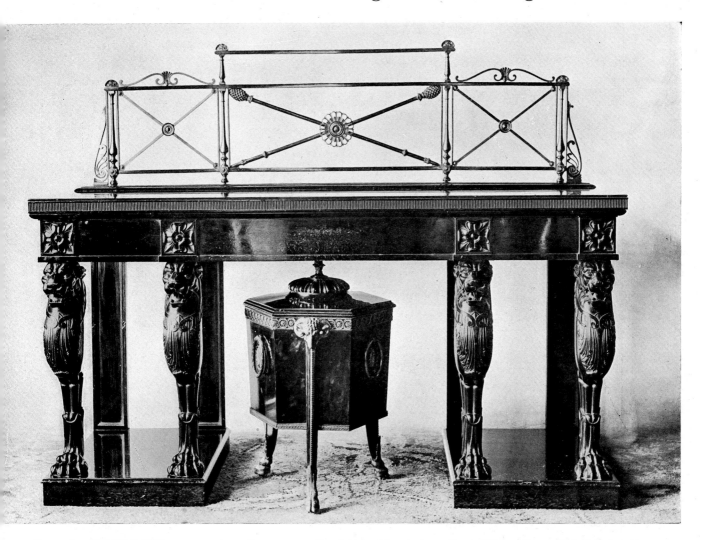

FIG. 163. SIDEBOARD supported on lion monopodia, fitted with a brass gallery. (The cellaret of earlier date.) *c.* 1815. From Balls Park.

FIG. 164. MAHOGANY SIDEBOARD supported on lion monopodia, fitted with a brass gallery; and sarcophagus-shaped cellaret. *c.* 1815. From the Marquess of Lansdowne, Bowood.

FIG. 165. MAHOGANY SIDEBOARD with carved bronzed enrichments and gallery. *c.* 1820. From Viscount Allendale, Bretton Park. Height, 4 feet 4½ inches. Length, 7 feet 10½ inches.

FIG. 166.
MAHOGANY CUPBOARD
with shelved superstructure
and doors fitted with a wire
trellis. From Kelvedon.

Height, 5 feet ½ inch.
Length, 6 feet 2½ inches.

FIG. 167. MAHOGANY PEDESTAL SIDEBOARD with shaped front. *c.* 1810 From Sir John Hall. Height, 3 feet 3 inches. Length 7 feet.

FIG. 168. MAHOGANY SIDEBOARD, shaped to fit an angle, and supported by lion monopodia. *c.* 1800. From J. F. Roxburgh, Esq.

FIG. 169. MAHOGANY SIDEBOARD inlaid with stringing lines. *c.* 1810. From Ralph Dutton, Esq., Hinton Ampner House. Height, 5 feet. Length, 8 feet 7½ inches.

FIG. 170. SIDEBOARD OR SIDETABLE the upper stage supported by Egyptian terms, the consoles and the upper stage and enrichments of the frieze of carved and gilt wood.

FIG. 171. MAHOGANY WINE TABLE, the drum containing japanned metal coasters and receptacles of Wedgwood ware. From the Marquess of Salisbury, Hatfield. Height, 2 feet 5 inches. Diameter, 3 feet 6 inches.

FIG. 172. MAHOGANY WINE COOLER with carved and gilt details. *c.* 1820. From the Town Hall Liverpool. Height, 2 feet 2 inches. Length, 3 feet 4 inches.

FIG. 173. MAHOGANY WINE COOLER mounted with gilt brass lion masks. *c.* 1797. From Castle Coole, Ireland.

FIG. 174. MAHOGANY WINE COOLER fitted with brass bands, tap, and lifting handles. Early 19th century. From the Pepys Cockerell Collection.

FIG. 175.
MAHOGANY DUMB WAITER inlaid with ebony, the lowest tier fitted with swinging holders for lights, the uppermost tier with hinged flaps. *c.* 1810.

. 176.
AHOGANY DUMB WAITER. Early 19th century. From Earl of Onslow, Clandon Park.

Ieight, 4 feet 11 inches.

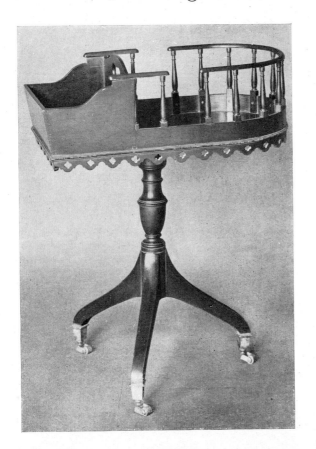

FIG. 177.
MAHOGANY PLATE STAND. From Denston Hall.

Height, 2 feet 3½ inches.
Length, 1 foot 11 inches.

FIG. 178.
MAHOGANY PLATE STAND on turned legs, the top divided with a partition for plates and partitions for cutlery. c. 1810.

FIG. 179.
TERRESTRIAL GLOBE on a mahogany stand, with carved lion supports. c. 1810. From Trinity House, London.

FIG. 180.
ROSEWOOD WHAT-NOT (one of a pair) mounted with ormolu.
c. 1800. From S. Whitbread, Esq., Southill.

FIG. 181.
STAND OR WHAT-NOT of black painted wood
inlaid with white, and with rings gilt, the lower part
fitted with two drawers, the top fitted with a marble
slab and brass gallery. (one of a pair.) From the Earl
Shaftesbury, St. Giles's House.

FIG. 182.
ROSEWOOD MUSIC STAND with wire trellis sides. c. 1815. From Sir John Hall.

Height, 2 feet 3½ inches.
Length, 2 feet.

FIG. 183.
MAHOGANY MUSIC DESK with adjustable top. c. 18

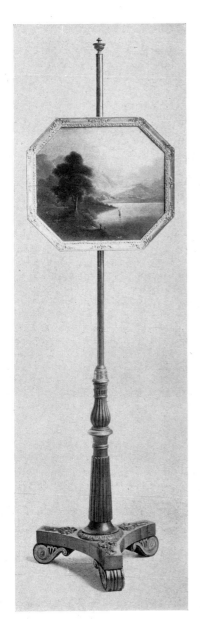

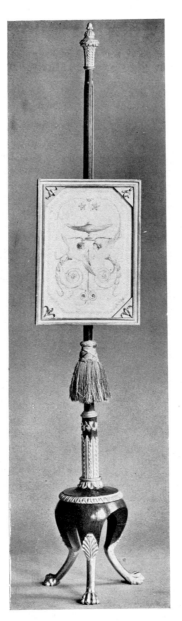

FIG. 184.
MAHOGANY POLE SCREEN
on flat triangular base framing
a landscape on an octagonal
frame. Early 19th century From
J. F. Roxburgh, Esq.

FIG. 185.
ROSEWOOD PANEL GILT
POLE SCREEN the panel
painted with arabesques in
water-colours by Delabriese.
c. 1800. From S. Whitbread,
Esq., Southill.

FIG. 186.
MAHOGANY TRIPOD POLE
SCREEN resting on reeded lion
paw feet. From James Thursby
Pelham, Esq.

FIG. 187. GILT CHIMNEY MIRROR, framing in the upper part a painting of ships at sea. Early 19th century. From Alveston House.

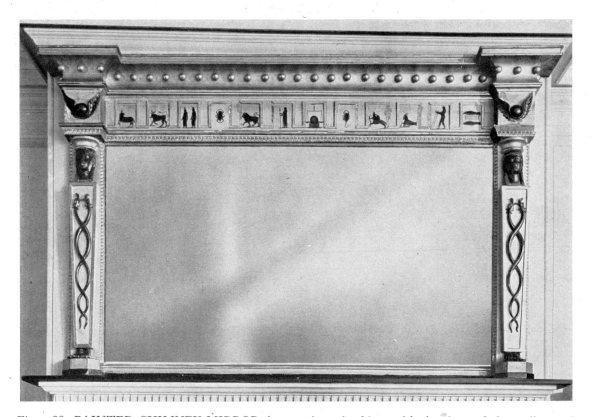

Fig. 188. PAINTED CHIMNEY MIRROR decorated on the frieze with the signs of the zodiac, and flanked by Egyptian terms. *c.* 1807. From Dixton Manor. Height, 3 feet 1 inch. Width 5 feet 8 inches.

Fig. 189. CHIMNEY MIRROR in gilt frame. *c.* 1800. From Major-General Sir Wilkinson Bird.

Fig. 190. CHIMNEY MIRROR in gilt frame, the frieze mounted with small convex mirrors and figures and groups in relief. *c.* 1800.

FIG. 191. CONVEX MIRROR in gilt wood frame, with reeded and ebonised inner moulding and having as a finial the crest of the Merchant Taylors' Company. *c.* 1795. From Merchant Taylors' Hall. Height, 7 feet 6 inches (to top of finial). Width, 6 feet 6 inches.

Fig. 192.
CONVEX MIRROR in gilt wood frame, the inner mouldings ebonised. *c.* 1800.

Height (to top of eagle), 2 feet 9 inches.

. 193.
NVEX MIRROR in gilt wood frame, the inner moulding nised. *c.* 1800. From the Victoria and Albert Museum.

Ieight, 8 feet 4 inches.

Fig. 194. MIRROR in carved and gilt frame, surmounted by a Greek pediment. *c.* 1810. From Sir Roderick and Lady Jones.

FIG. 195.
BRONZE HANGING LAMP with gilt enrichments, dated 1817.
From Humphrey Whitbread, Esq.

196.
ANDELIER of metal and cut glass. *c.* 1800. From
dle's Club.

FIG. 197.
BRONZE HANGING LAMP for two burners, with gilt enrichments. Early 19th century. From Denston Hall.

Length, 1 foot, 10 inches.

FIG. 198.
BRONZE HANGING LAMP for four burners. *c.* 1800. From Lord Methuen, Corsham Court.

Height, 4 feet 7 inches.

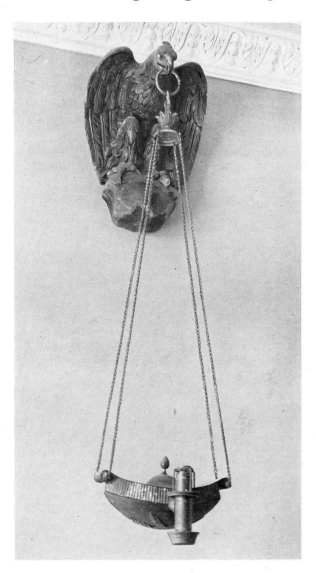

FIG. 199.
HANGING LAMP for one burner, suspended from a carved and gilt eagle. From Crawley House, Aspley Guise.

FIG. 200.
BRONZE LAMP with gilt brass enrichments. *c.* 1810. From the Earl of Caledon, Caledon, Ireland.

Diameter of bowl, 12½ inches.

Lighting Fittings

FIG. 201.
HANGING LAMP with cut glass base, metal vase, burners and chains. Early 19th century. From Ralph Dutton, Esq., Hinton Ampner House.

Diameter of base, 1 foot 10¾ inches.

FIG. 202.
BRONZE HANGING LAMP with gilt brass enrichments. Early 19th century.

Width between arms, 1 foot 8½ inches.

Fig. 203.
CARVED AND GILT WALL LIGHT for one candle.
From Halnaby Hall.

   Length, 1 foot 11½ inches.

Fig. 204.
GILT WALL LIGHT for two candles, centring
in an oval convex mirror. Early 19th century.
From Colonel and Mrs. Jenner.

   Length 2 feet 6½ inches.

FIG. 206. SILVER-GILT CANDELABRUM for seven lights, in the Egyptian taste. Made by Smith & Sharp for the Duke of Cumberland in 1805. Height, 3 feet.

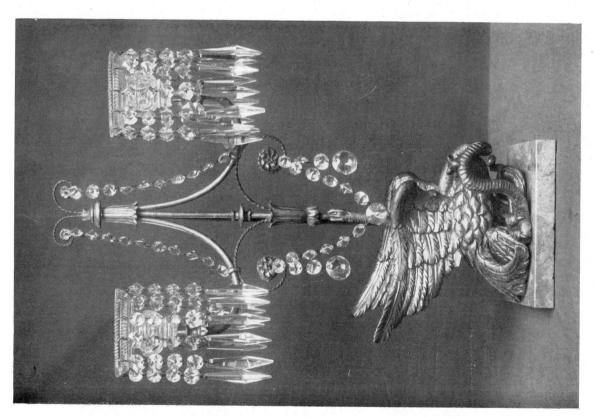

FIG. 205. CANDELABRUM of gilt brass hung with cut glass.

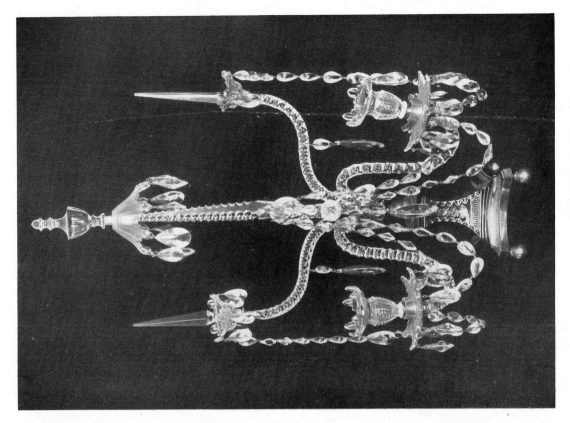

Fig. 208. CUT-GLASS CANDELABRUM

Fig. 207. CUT-GLASS CANDELABRUM with porcelain base.

Lighting Fittings

FIG. 209.
CANDLESTICK with cut glass drum and gilt brass stem, fitted with a bell-shaped ground glass shade painted in the Chinese taste. *c.* 1810. From Basil Ionides, Esq., Buxted Park.

Height, 1 foot 3¼ inches.
Diameter of top, 6¾ inches.

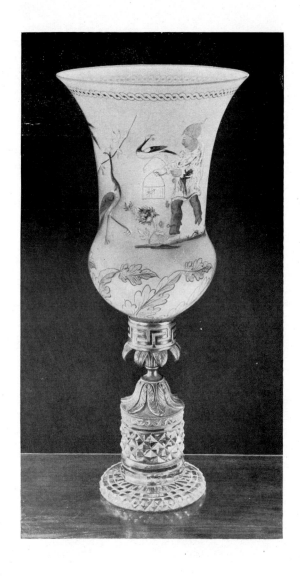

FIG. 210.
CUT-GLASS CANDLESTICK with base of blue and white Wedgwood ware. *c.* 1800. From the Victoria and Albert Museum.

FIG. 211.
CANDLESTICK with glass base and clear-glass shade.

IG. 212.
HEFFIELD PLATE CANDLESTICK
ith painted glass shade. *c.* 1825.

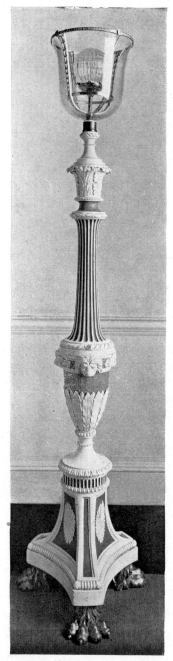

FIG. 213.
CARVED AND PAINTED
LAMP-STAND. *c.* 1795.
From Mrs. Hamlyn, Clovelly
Court.

Height, 6 feet.

FIG. 214.
GILT METAL LAMP on a columnar support
resting on a mahogany pedestal. Early 19th
century. From the Duke of Northumberland,
Syon House.

Height, 8 feet 10 inches.

FIG. 215. MAHOGANY WARDROBE in the Egyptian taste. *c.* 1807. Height, 7 feet 9 inches. Width, 4 feet 5½ inches.

Fig. 216. A FOUR-POST CANOPIED AND DOMED BED. Early 19th century. From Wimpole Hall.

FIG. 217. SATINWOOD DRESSING TABLE inlaid with ebony. Designed by
George Smith and illustrated in his *Household Furniture* (see Fig. 233). *c.* 1808.
Height, 2 feet 4 inches. Length, 3 feet 11 inches. Depth, 1 foot 11¾ inches.

FIG. 218. MAHOGANY CHEST OF DRAWERS with spirally-twisted columns at the
angles. *c.* 1815. From Denston Hall. Height, 3 feet 6 inches. Length, 3 feet 8 inches.

FIG. 219.
SATINWOOD CHEVAL GLASS inlaid and banded
with zebra wood. *c.* 1800. From Mrs. Stileman.

FIG. 220.
MAHOGANY CHEVAL GLASS the standards headed with
Egyptian terminal figures. *c.* 1807.

Height, 5 feet 8½ inches.
Width, 2 feet 10 inches.
Depth, 2 feet 3½ inches.

FIG. 221. SATINWOOD DRESSING TABLE AND DRESSING GLASS. (Made by George Oakley in 1810.) From Mrs. Stileman. Height (including mirror), 5 feet. Length, 4 feet 6 inches.

FIG. 222. ROSEWOOD DRESSING TABLE AND GLASS, the table mounted
with French ormolu classical heads and having applied brass mouldings to the
frieze. *c.* 1805. From the Duke of Wellington.

FIG. 223.
MAHOGANY DRESSING MIRROR with an oblong glass supported on balusters fixed to a box stand. *c.* 1800.

Height, 1 foot 10¼ inches.

FIG. 224.
MAHOGANY DRESSING MIRROR supported on turned balusters, fixed to a box stand and resting on globular feet of ivory.

FIG. 225. MIRROR ON WALNUT TRIPOD STAND. *ɔ.* 1815. From the Thomas-Stanford Museum, Brighton. Height 5 feet 6 inches (to top of mirror).

FIG. 226. BED, with curtains and valances of painted silk surmounted by the Prince of Wales's plume of feathers. *c.* 1810. From Ragley Hall.

FIG. 227. GRAINED CHEST OF DRAWERS with bamboo mouldings. From Sir Roderick and Lady Jones.

FIG. 228. DESIGN FOR A LIBRARY TABLE. From Sheraton's
Encyclopaedia (1805).

FIG. 229. DESIGN FOR A WRITING-TABLE in the Egyptian taste. From George
Smith's *Household Furniture* (1808).

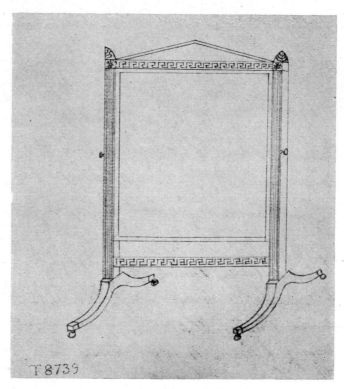

FIG. 230. A SCREEN DRESSING GLASS. From Gillow's books (1807).

FIG. 231. DESIGN FOR A DRUM-TOPPED TABLE. *c.* 1800. From Gillow's Cost books.

FIG. 232. DESIGN FOR CYLINDER WRITING-TABLE. From Sheraton's *Cabinet Dictionary* (1803).

FIG. 233. DESIGN FOR A DRESSING TABLE. From George Smith's *Household Furniture* (1808). (See Fig. 217.)

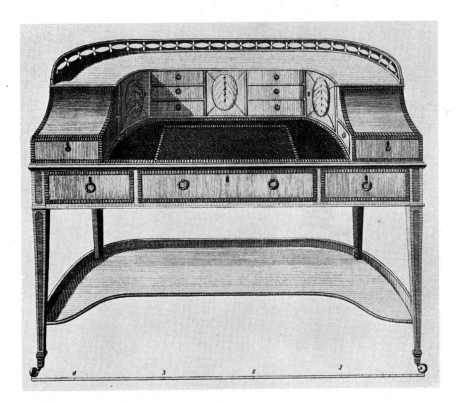

FIG. 234. DESIGN FOR A 'LADY'S DRAWING AND WRITING TABLE' (of 'Carlton House' type). From Sheraton's *Cabinet-makers' and Upholsterers' Drawing Book* (1791–1794).

FIG. 235. DESIGN FOR A STAND FOR A LAMP by
Henry Holland. *c.* 1790. From the Royal Institute of British
Architects.

Index

Index

Index

Index